Java with the
Judges

Advancing the Ministries of the Gospel
AMG *Publishers*

God's Word to you is our highest calling.

SANDRA GLAHN

Coffee Cup Bible Studies
Java with the Judges

© 2006 by Sandra L. Glahn

Published by AMG Publishers. All Rights Reserved.

Published in association with the literary
agency of Alive Communications, Inc., 7860 Goddard Street, Suite 200,
Colorado Springs, Colorado, 80920

First Printing, 2006

ISBN: 0-89957-221-9

Editing and Proofreading: Rick Steele and Jonathan Wright
Interior Design: PerfecType, Nashville, Tennessee
Cover Design: Brian Woodlief at ImageWright Marketing and Design,
Chattanooga, Tennessee

Printed in the United States of America
11 10 09   –D– 6 5 4 3 2

ACKNOWLEDGMENTS

During my seminary training I took a class during which I was given the assignment to consider the leadership example of Nehemiah. Each student was given a different chapter to explore, and I ended up with Nehemiah 3. Frankly, I thought I got the worst pick (if one dare say such a thing about the Bible). The entire chapter of Nehemiah 3 is taken up in listing Eliashib and Meriboth and everyone else who helped rebuild the city walls. I found it almost amusing that the citations even included the perfume workers' guild. (See Nehemiah 3:8). What could I possibly learn about leadership from long lists of difficult-to-pronounce names?

Then it dawned on me: Nobody who accomplishes a major ministry task does so alone. And anyone who fails to acknowledge "I couldn't have done this by myself" is probably suffering from a serious case of hubris.

I most certainly did not write this study without help. And so, I would like to especially thank the following:

- to Gary, my husband, for his tireless, loyal love and for believing I could teach and write occupationally long before I had any vision to do so. To Gary goes additional thanks for designing and keeping up with the web site parts of the Coffee Cup series

- to Dr. Bob Chisholm for making Hebrew narrative—especially Judges and Ruth—come alive with the help of a little stand-up comedy

- to Alison, Barb, Beth, Daena, Debbie, Dena, Emily, Erin, Jeni, Jennifer, Judy, Julia, Kelley, Linda, Lisa, Mary, Sylba, Yvonne, and the entire "test group" at Creekside, now Rowlett Bible Fellowship, for their terrific feedback and their involvement with this study, starting with their creation and performance of "Here Come Da Judges." (Our apologies to the late Sammy Davis, Jr.)

- to Keith Yates for lending his artistic skills in providing the illustrations

- to Chip MacGregor, my former agent turned publisher, for helping me hone the series concept and finding a home for it

- to Virginia Swint and Karen Swint for always being available with extra sets of proofers' eyes

- to Rhonda Oglesby and Erin Teske for providing a means by which readers can give artistic expression to their contemplations at www.soulpersuit.com

- to the gifted staff of Biblical Studies Press (bible.org), translators of the NET Bible translation printed as the primary Scripture text in this book. Without the help of this essential ministry, the entire concept of the Coffee Cup Bible Studies would not be possible

- to Dan Penwell and Rick Steele of AMG for their enthusiasm for the project, their commitment to excellence, and their generous encouragement along the way

- to those who are praying that lives will be changed through interaction with the biblical text. You know who you are

- to the Lord Jesus Christ, apart from whom none of us can do anything

INTRODUCTION TO THE
COFFEE CUP BIBLE STUDIES

"The precepts of the LORD are right, rejoicing the heart;
The commandment of the LORD is pure, enlightening the eyes." (Psa. 19:8, NASB)

Congratulations! You have chosen wisely. By choosing to study the Bible, you are electing to spend time learning that which will rejoice the heart and enlighten the eyes.

And while any study in the Bible is time well spent, the Coffee Cup Bible series has some unique elements that set it apart from others. So before we get started, let's talk about some of those elements that will, we hope, help you maximize your study time.

Life Rhythms. Most participants in any Bible study have little problem keeping up during the weekdays, when they have a routine. Yet on the weekends there's a general "falling off." Thus, the *Coffee Cup Bible Studies* contain Monday-through-Friday Bible study questions, but the Saturday and Sunday segments consist of short more passive readings that draw application and insight from the texts you'll be considering. Know that the days listed here are mere suggestions. Feel free to change the structure of days and assignments to best fit your own needs.

Community. The studies in the Coffee Cup series are ideal for group interaction. If you don't have a local group with which to meet, find a few friends and start one. Or connect with others through the Esther section of the author's web site (www.aspire2.com) and an

v

associated site, where you can find and participate—if you like—by engaging in artistic expressions as you interact with the text. These vehicles give you opportunities to share with a wider community what you're learning. While each study is designed for group use, private questions not intended for group discussion appear in italics.

Aesthetics. At the author's web site a section designed for association with the Coffee Cup Bible Studies provides links to art that depicts what's being discussed—from one of Rembrandt's depictions of Boaz and Ruth, to one of Gustave Doré's many works illustrating stories from the period of the judges, to some of the many contemporary works. And as mentioned, readers who want to engage all five senses in their interaction with God's truth will find a link to a site set up for encouraging that very purpose.

Convenience. Rather than turning in the Bible to find the references, you'll find the entire text for each day included in the Coffee Cup study book. While it's important to know our way around the Bible, the Coffee Cup series is designed this way so you can take it with you and study the Bible on the subway or at a coffee shop or in a doctors' waiting room or on your lunch break. The chosen translation is the NET Bible, which is accessible via internet from virtually anywhere in the world. You can find more about it, along with numerous textual notes, at www.bible.org, which serves 3.5 million people worldwide.

The NET Bible is a modern translation from the ancient Greek, Hebrew, and Aramaic texts. Alumni and friends of Dallas Theological Seminary make up the core group of individuals behind the site, particularly the NET Bible translation project. Both the online and text versions of this Bible include 60,932 translators' notes and citations pulling from more than 700 scholarly works.

Sensitivity to time-and-culture considerations. Many Bible studies skip what we call the "theological" step. That is, they go straight from observing and interpreting the words given to those in a different time and culture to applying them to a modern-day setting. The result is sometimes misapplication (such as, "Paul told slaves to obey their *masters* so we need to obey our *employers*"). In the Coffee Cup series, our aim is to be particularly sensitive to the audience to whom the "mail" was addressed and work to take the crucial step of separating what was intended for a limited audience from that which is for all audiences for all time (love God; love your neighbor).

Sensitivity to genres. Rather than crafting a series in which each study is structured exactly like all the others, each Coffee Cup Bible Series study is structured to best consider the genre being examined— whether poetry, gospel, history, or narrative. The way we study Esther, a story, differs from how someone might study Paul's epistle to the Ephesians or the poetry in Song of Songs. So while the studies may have similar elements, no two will be quite the same.

INTRODUCTION TO JAVA WITH THE JUDGES

"Everyone did what was right in his own eyes." Sound familiar? In the history of the nation of Israel, the period of the judges was a lot like today. Maybe they didn't have Internet porn and bio-terrorism threats, but they had the me-centered "I" problem mastered—just like we do. As a result, they kept getting themselves oppressed by other nations. Then God would raise judges to deliver them. This chart will show you the book of Judges at a glance.

This study is chock full of exciting drama—from Ehud the Knifer to Samson the Seduced to Deborah the Leader. Their stories—whether by negative or positive example—can inspire us to do what is right in God's eyes no matter what the cost. Because Hannah's story takes place during the time of the judges, an overview of the first few chapters of 1 Samuel is also included.

Judge	Israel's Oppressors		Length of Years	
	Nations	King(s)	Oppression	Peace
Othniel	Mesopotamia	Cushan–rishathaim	8	40
Ehud Ammon Amalek	Moab	Eglon	18	80
Shamgar	Philistia			
Deborah	Canaan	Jabin	20	40
Gideon	Midian Amalek Arabia	Zeba Zalmunna	7	40
Tola				Judged 23 years
Jair				Judged 22 years
Jephthah	Ammon		18	Judged 6 years
Ibzan				Judged 7 years
Elon				Judged 10 years
Abdon				Judged 8 years
Samson	Philistia		40	Judged 20 years

CONTENTS

THE TIME OF THE JUDGES

To understand what's happening in the Book of Judges, it's important to consider a short history of Israel. Thousands of years before the events in this book take place, Abram, though childless, receives a promise from God that he will become a great nation (see Genesis 12). God keeps His promise, but eventually the descendants of Abraham go to Egypt. Joseph's family follows him there during a famine, and they stay, multiply, and eventually became slaves.

About four hundred seventy years after Joseph, Moses leads the people through the Red Sea and back to their original country—the Promised Land. If you've read Exodus or seen *The Prince of Egypt,* you know the story. After that, Moses' followers don't have "forty days of purpose." Rather, they have "forty years of wandering aimlessly." Finally Moses appoints Joshua as his successor and dies.

Under Joshua's able leadership, Israel marches into the Promised Land. After many successful military campaigns, Israel generally subdues the pagan people, and God's people stand clearly in charge. When Joshua retires after a long, successful career, the nation's future looks fabulous. It doesn't take long, though, for optimism to turn to despair.

The nation, having fallen short of completely annihilating the Canaanites as God had commanded, face the consequences of their failure to obey completely.

The situation: the disobedience of God's people plunges the nation into a downward cycle, repeated over and over in the Book of Judges. The cycle looks something like this:

The Cycle of Misery

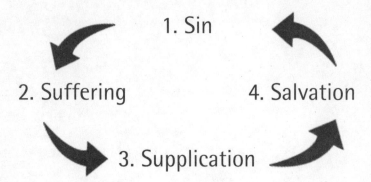

1. Sin

2. Suffering

4. Salvation

3. Supplication

It may strike us as rather gory for God to tell His people to destroy other humans (Deut. 7:1–6; Josh. 6:17–21). Yet three observations help us understand His command:

1. The land was God's gift from God to Abraham. His people were re-conquering their own territory.

2. God had put up with the Canaanites for 400 years—that's twice as long as the entire history of the United States. Yet they had blindly refused His grace and sunk deeper and deeper into evil practices.

3. The Canaanites were horrible. The Bible presents them in the darkest possible terms. They sacrificed humans, indulged in orgies, worshiped demons, and engaged in other practices too repulsive to describe here. They celebrated cruelty and made defilement part of their religion. Consider how the land's inhabitants are described in the following verses:

> **Leviticus 18:21** "'You must not give any of your children as offspring to Molech, so that you do not profane the name of your God. I am the Lord!
>
> **22** "'Do not have sexual intercourse with a male as one has sexual intercourse with a woman; it is a detestable act.

23 "'You must not have sexual intercourse with any animal to become defiled with it, and a woman must not stand before an animal to have sexual intercourse with it; it is a perversion.

24 "'Do not defile yourselves with any of these things, for the nations (which I am about to drive out before you) have been defiled with all these things.

25 Therefore the land has become unclean and I have brought the punishment it for its iniquity on it, so that the land has vomited out its inhabitants.

Deuteronomy 12:29 When the Lord your God eliminates the nations from the place where you are headed and you dispossess them, you will settle down in their land.

30 After they have been destroyed from your presence, be careful not to be ensnared like they are; do not pursue their gods and say, "How do these nations serve their gods? I will do the same."

31 You must not worship the Lord your God the way they do! For everything that is abhorrent to him, everything he hates, they have done when worshiping their gods. They even burn up their sons and daughters before their gods!

32 You must be careful to do everything I am commanding you. Do not add to it nor subtract from it!

The Canaanites were bad news. And we see in the Book of Judges the consequences of failing to obey God's command to drive them out.

In terms of Israel's internal affairs, the greatest contrast between the last days of Joshua and the period of the judges is in the quality of its leadership. This period fell from approximately 1220 BC to 1050 BC. It is God's intention that His people look to Him for leadership in the absence of a formal government or monarchy. The people's disobedience, however, kept them in a repeating cycle of sin, suffering, supplication, and salvation.

We should note that the various oppressions did not necessarily involve the entire nation each time. Also, some of the judges' time periods may have overlapped, and there may have been some years during which there was no judge at all.

Who wrote the book? As is often the case with Old Testament books, the writer of the book remains anonymous. We do know that its author lived after kings began to rule in Israel (Judg. 17:6; 18:1; 19:1; 21:25).

What was a judge? Today in modern North America we think of a judge as a person who presides in court; however, judges in those days were often both judicial officials and military leaders or clan chieftains. They appeared from time to time in different areas among Israel's tribes (see map below for a few examples), often bringing deliverance from enemies who threatened parts of the nation. Several judges, such as Samson, were deeply flawed. Thus, we see once again how the God who made elaborate promises to Abraham about his descendants kept those promises because of His compassion and long-suffering despite the continuing rebellion of His people.

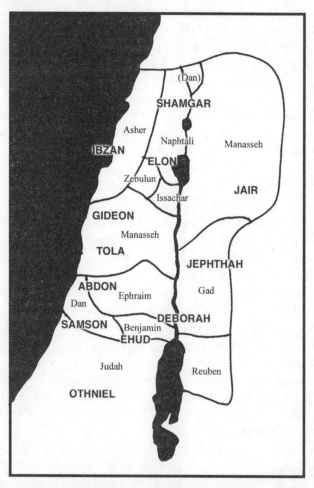

Map of Israel During the Period of the Judges
(Judges appear in all caps. Tribes of Israel appear in lighter type)

WEEK 1 OF 6

The Good Guys: Judges 1—3

Scripture: "Caleb said, 'To the man who attacks and captures Kiriath Sepher I will give my daughter Acsah as a wife.'" (Judges 1:12)

After ten years of infertility, which included seven pregnancy losses and three failed adoptions for us, my husband and I were finally parents. Ecstatic parents.

The first day we had our daughter, my husband announced that he wasn't letting her date until she turned twenty-one.

By the second day, he had raised her date of eligibility to age thirty-five.

On the third day, a friend shook his head and told me, "You'd better try to stop the trend now, or you'll never be grandparents."

Up to that time, the idea of arranged marriages had seemed ridiculous to us. What could parents possibly know about making their kids happy at love? Yet suddenly once we were parents, we realized we might know a thing or two more about what makes love last than our daughter would as a teen, or even as a young woman.

1

How much difference one day can make!

Not so many years ago, parents arranged marriages for their children. In fact, "Until 200 years ago, courtship was not typically conducted at dinners by candlelight or trysts under the moon, but negotiated by parents, cousins, neighbors and lawyers in the light of day. People married to consummate a property transaction or political alliance, or to work a farm together. A wedding was not the happy ending to a passionate romance. It was often the unhappy ending to one partner's romance with someone else."[1]

Back when I was in high school, someone asked what I thought of arranged marriages. I pictured my parents choosing me a guy in a business suit with greased back hair and geek glasses. Being more interested in football players and rock musicians, I laughed at the thought.

I ended up marrying a guy who paved roads for a living and wore really cool patched jeans. That was fine, but I actually didn't mind so much when he went on to wear business suits and to work for a law firm. In an interesting twist, both my parents and I are happy.

And as it turns out, parents aren't always as clueless as I had thought. Interestingly enough, studies tell us that couples in arranged marriages actually have a decent chance of ending up happier than a lot of us who got to choose.

So should we arrange marriages for our kids?

Uh, no. That's definitely not my point. For one thing, I wouldn't want my daughter calling me to argue by saying, "Hey, you're the one who made me marry this guy."

But here's my point: We have to be careful, very careful, about reading our own cultural practices and values into the biblical text and our understanding of what was happening at the time it was written. Otherwise, our interpretations and applications may be way off.

Case in point: In the Book of Judges we have Caleb, Moses' successor. Caleb is a hero—one of a select group of spies who actually trusts God no matter how bleak the circumstances. But suddenly we find our hero offering his daughter's hand in marriage as a prize in a conquest.

What? What's wrong with him? Does he think she's property or something?

---

[1] *Stephanie Coontz*, "Historically Incorrect Canoodling" *New York Times*, February 14, 2005. Available at http://stephaniecoontz.com/articles/article11.htm, accessed January 11, 2006.

Well, actually yes—and no.

In Caleb's day, men did consider women, along with cattle and sheep, as their possessions. But we have to remember that the culture and practices were not inspired. Only God's Words are inspired.

Nevertheless, Caleb isn't offering his daughter because of some power trip for his own ego gratification. He's not offering her as a political alliance between warring parties. And he's not offering her to make money. In the past, parents have done each of these. But not Caleb. He's seeking for his girl a man who is valiant in battle (important when there's no police force), and more importantly one who has the courage and faith to obey God's command to conquer.

So, yes, we've come a long way, baby. I'm glad I got to choose the love of my life. But still, when we read Judges, we can see that perhaps the starting point wasn't as far back as we might have thought. Our neighbors, Christians whose marriage was arranged, tell us you can grow to love anyone as a partner if he or she has the fruit of the Spirit.

MONDAY: CALEB AND THE FIRST THREE JUDGES

1. Ask for the Spirit's insight, and then read the first three chapters of Judges, preferably all in one sitting. It's shorter than a major news story.

Judges 1

1:1 After Joshua died, the Israelites asked the Lord, "Who should lead the invasion against the Canaanites and launch the attack?" **1:2** The Lord said, "The men of Judah should take the lead. Be sure of this! I am handing the land over to them." **1:3** The men of Judah said to their brothers, the men of Simeon, "Invade our allotted land with us and help us attack the Canaanites. Then we will go with you into your allotted land." So the men of Simeon went with them.

1:4 The men of Judah attacked, and the Lord handed the Canaanites and Perizzites over to them. They killed ten thousand men at Bezek. **1:5** They met Adoni-Bezek at Bezek and fought him. They defeated the Canaanites and Perizzites. **1:6** When Adoni-Bezek ran away, they chased him and captured him. Then they cut off his thumbs and big toes. **1:7** Adoni-Bezek said, "Seventy kings, with thumbs and big toes cut off, used to lick up food scraps under my table. God has repaid me for what I did to them." They brought him to Jerusalem, where he died. **1:8** The men of Judah attacked Jerusalem and captured it. They put the sword to it and set the city on fire.

1:9 Later the men of Judah went down to attack the Canaanites living in the hill country, the Negev, and the lowlands. **1:10** The men of Judah attacked the Canaanites living in Hebron. (Hebron used to be

> *Judges 1:6–7 states that Adoni-Bezek endured some amputations. Cutting off thumbs and big toes both humiliated captives and rendered them incapable of using weapons.*

called Kiriath Arba.) They killed Sheshai, Ahiman, and Talmai. **1:11** From there they attacked the people of Debir. (Debir used to be called Kiriath Sepher.) **1:12** Caleb said, "To the man who attacks and captures Kiriath Sepher I will give my daughter Acsah as a wife." **1:13** When Othniel son of Kenaz, Caleb's younger brother, captured it, Caleb gave him his daughter Acsah as a wife.

1:14 One time Acsah came and charmed her father so she could ask him for some land. When she got down from her donkey, Caleb said to her, "What would you like?" **1:15** She answered, "Please give me a special present. Since you have given me land in the Negev, now give me springs of water." So Caleb gave her both the upper and lower springs.

1:16 Now the descendants of the Kenite, Moses' father-in-law, went up with the people of Judah from the City of Date Palm Trees to Arad in the desert of Judah, located in the Negev. They went and lived with the people of Judah.

1:17 The men of Judah went with their brothers the men of Simeon and defeated the Canaanites living in Zephath. They wiped out Zephath. So people now call the city Hormah. **1:18** The men of Judah captured Gaza, Ashkelon, Ekron, and the territory surrounding each of these cities.

1:19 The Lord was with the men of Judah. They conquered the hill country, but they could not conquer the people living in the coastal plain, because they had chariots with iron-rimmed wheels. **1:20** Caleb received Hebron, just as Moses had promised. He drove out the three Anakites. **1:21** The men of Benjamin, however, did not conquer the Jebusites living in Jerusalem. The Jebusites live with the people of Benjamin in Jerusalem to this very day.

1:22 When the men of Joseph attacked Bethel, the Lord was with them. **1:23** When the men of Joseph spied out Bethel (it used to be called Luz), **1:24** the spies spotted a man leaving the city. They said to him, "If you show us a secret entrance into the city, we will reward you." **1:25** He showed them a secret entrance into the city, and they put the city to the sword. But they let the man and his extended family leave safely. **1:26** He moved to Hittite country and built a city. He named it Luz, and it has kept that name to this very day.

1:27 The men of Manasseh did not conquer Beth Shan, Taanach, or their surrounding towns. Nor did they conquer the people living in Dor, Ibleam, Megiddo or their surrounding towns. The Canaanites managed to remain in those areas. **1:28** Whenever Israel was strong militarily, they forced the Canaanites to do hard labor, but they never totally conquered them.

1:29 The men of Ephraim did not conquer the Canaanites living in Gezer. The Canaanites lived among them in Gezer.

1:30 The men of Zebulun did not conquer the people living in Kitron and Nahalol. The Canaanites lived among them and were forced to do hard labor.

1:31 The men of Asher did not conquer the people living in Acco or Sidon. Nor did they conquer Ahlab, Aczib, Helbah, Aphek, or Rehob. **1:32** The people of Asher live among the Canaanites residing in the land because they did not conquer them.

1:33 The men of Naphtali did not conquer the people living in Beth Shemesh or Beth Anath. They live among the Canaanites residing in the land. The Canaanites living in Beth Shemesh and Beth Anath were forced to do hard labor for them.

1:34 The Amorites forced the people of Dan to live in the hill country. They did not allow them to live in the coastal plain. **1:35** The Amorites managed to remain in Har Heres, Aijalon, and Shaalbim. Whenever the tribe of Joseph was strong militarily, the Amorites were forced to do hard labor. **1:36** The border of Amorite territory ran from the Ascent of Aqrabbim to Sela and on up.

Judges 2

2:1 The Lord's angelic messenger went up from Gilgal to Bokim. He said, "I brought you up from Egypt and led you into the land I had solemnly promised to give to your ancestors. I said, 'I will never break my agreement with you, **2:2** but you must not make an agreement with the people who live in this land. You should tear down the altars where they worship.' But you have disobeyed me. Why would you do such a thing? **2:3** At that time I also warned you,

'If you disobey, I will not drive out the Canaanites before you. They will ensnare you and their gods will lure you away.'"

2:4 When the Lord's messenger finished speaking these words to all the Israelites, the people wept loudly. **2:5** They named that place Bokim and offered sacrifices to the Lord there.

2:6 When Joshua dismissed the people, the Israelites went to their allotted portions of property, intending to take possession of the land. **2:7** The people worshiped the Lord throughout Joshua's lifetime and as long as the elderly men who outlived him remained alive. These men had witnessed all the great things the Lord had done for Israel. **2:8** Joshua son of Nun, the Lord's servant, died at the age of one hundred and ten. **2:9** The people buried him in his allotted land in Timnath Heres in the hill country of Ephraim, north of Mount Gaash. **2:10** That entire generation passed away; a new generation came along that had not personally experienced the Lord's presence or seen what he had done for Israel.

2:11 The Israelites did evil before the Lord by worshiping the Baals. **2:12** They abandoned the Lord God of their ancestors who brought them out of the land of Egypt. They followed other gods—the gods of the nations who lived around them. They worshiped them and made the Lord angry. **2:13** They abandoned the Lord and worshiped Baal and the Ashtars.

2:14 The Lord was furious with Israel and handed them over to robbers who plundered them. He turned them over to their enemies who lived around them. They could not withstand their enemies' attacks. **2:15** Whenever they went out to fight, the Lord did them harm, just as he had warned and solemnly vowed he would do. They suffered greatly.

2:16 The Lord raised up leaders who delivered them from these robbers. **2:17** But they did not obey their leaders. Instead they prostituted themselves to other gods and worshiped them. They quickly turned aside from the path their ancestors had walked. Their ancestors had obeyed the Lord's commands, but they did not. **2:18** When the Lord raised up leaders for them, the Lord was with each leader and delivered the people from their enemies while the leader remained alive. The Lord felt sorry for them when they cried out in agony because of what their harsh oppressors did to them. **2:19** When a leader died, the next generation would again act more wickedly than the previous one. They would follow after other gods, worshiping them and bowing down to them. They did not give up their practices or their stubborn ways.

2:20 The Lord was furious with Israel. He said, "This nation has violated the terms of the agreement I made with their ancestors by disobeying me. **2:21** So I will no longer remove before them any of the nations that Joshua left unconquered when he died. **2:22** Joshua left those nations to test Israel. I wanted to see whether or not the people would carefully walk in the path marked out by the Lord, as their ancestors were careful to do." **2:23** This is why the Lord permitted these nations to remain and did not conquer them immediately; he did not hand them over to Joshua.

Judges 3

3:1 These were the nations the Lord permitted to remain so he could use them to test Israel—he wanted to test all those who had not experienced battle against the Canaanites. **3:2** He left those nations simply because he wanted to teach the subsequent generations of Israelites, who had not experienced the earlier battles, how to conduct holy war. **3:3** These were the nations: the five lords of the Philistines, all the Canaanites, the Sidonians, and the Hivites living in Mount Lebanon, from Mount Baal Hermon to Lebo-Hamath. **3:4** They were left to test Israel, so the Lord would know if his people would obey the commands he gave their ancestors through Moses.

3:5 The Israelites lived among the Canaanites, Hittites, Amorites, Perizzites, Hivites, and Jebusites. **3:6** They took the Canaanites' daughters as wives and gave their daughters to the Canaanites; they worshiped their gods as well.

3:7 The Israelites did evil in the Lord's sight. They forgot the Lord their God and worshiped the Baals and the Asherahs. **3:8** The Lord was furious with Israel and turned them over to King Cushan-Rishathaim of Aram-Naharaim. They were Cushan-Rishathaim's subjects for eight years. **3:9** When the Israelites cried out for help to the Lord, he raised up a deliverer for the Israelites who rescued them. His name was Othniel son of Kenaz, Caleb's younger brother. **3:10** The Lord's spirit empowered him and he led Israel. When he went to do battle, the Lord handed over to him King Cushan-Rishathaim of Aram and he overpowered him. **3:11** The land had rest for forty years; then Othniel son of Kenaz died.

3:12 The Israelites again did evil in the Lord's sight. The Lord gave King Eglon of Moab control over Israel because they had done evil in the Lord's sight. **3:13** Eglon allied with the Ammonites and Amalekites. He came and defeated Israel, and they seized the City of

Date Palm Trees. **3:14** The Israelites were subject to King Eglon of Moab for eighteen years.

3:15 When the Israelites cried out for help to the Lord, he raised up a deliverer for them. His name was Ehud son of Gera the Benjaminite, a left-handed man. The Israelites sent him to King Eglon of Moab with their tribute payment. **3:16** Ehud made himself a sword—it had two edges and was eighteen inches long. He strapped it under his coat on his right thigh. **3:17** He brought the tribute payment to King Eglon of Moab. (Now Eglon was a very fat man.)

3:18 After Ehud brought the tribute payment, he dismissed the people who had carried it. **3:19** But he went back once he reached the carved images at Gilgal. He said to Eglon, "I have a secret message for you, O king." Eglon said, "Be quiet!" All his attendants left. **3:20** When Ehud approached him, he was sitting in his well-ventilated upper room all by himself. Ehud said, "I have a divine message for you." When Eglon rose up from his seat, **3:21** Ehud reached with his left hand, pulled the sword from his right thigh, and drove it into Eglon's belly. **3:22** The handle went in after the blade, and the fat closed around the blade, for Ehud did not pull the sword out of his belly. **3:23** As Ehud went out into the vestibule, he closed the doors of the upper room behind him and locked them.

3:24 When Ehud had left, Eglon's servants came and saw the locked doors of the upper room. They said, "He must be relieving himself in the well-ventilated inner room." **3:25** They waited so long they were embarrassed, but he still did not open the doors of the upper room. Finally they took the key and opened the doors. Right before their eyes was their master, sprawled out dead on the floor! **3:26** Now Ehud had escaped while they were delaying. When he passed the carved images, he escaped to Seirah.

3:27 When he reached Seirah, he blew a trumpet in the Ephraimite hill country. The Israelites went down with him from the hill country, with Ehud in the lead. **3:28** He said to them, "Follow me, for the Lord is about to defeat your enemies, the Moabites!" They followed him, captured the fords of the Jordan River opposite Moab, and did not let anyone cross. **3:29** That day they killed about ten thousand Moabites—all strong, capable warriors; not one escaped. **3:30** Israel humiliated Moab that day, and the land had rest for eighty years.

3:31 After Ehud came Shamgar son of Anath; he killed six hundred Philistines with an oxgoad and, like Ehud, delivered Israel.

2. After reading this, what questions do you have?

_____

_____

_____

_____

3. What observations or insights come to mind?

_____

_____

_____

TUESDAY: TRIBAL WARFARE

1. What is the first question in the book, which sets the stage? (Judg. 1:1.)

Who shall lead . . .

2. The twelve tribes of Israel are comprised of the offspring of Jacob's twelve sons, whose stories you can read in Genesis. Reuben, the oldest, lost his rights as a firstborn by sleeping with one of his father's concubines (see Gen. 35:22; 49:3–4). Taking Reuben's place are Joseph's two sons, Ephraim and Manassah (Gen. 48:5–6). So by this time in history the twelve tribes are as follows: Simeon, Levi, Judah, Issachar, Zebulun, Benjamin, Dan, Naphtali, Gad, Asher, Ephraim, and Manasseh. Read Judges 1:21, 27, 29, 30, 32 below.

> **Judges 1:21** The men of Benjamin, however, did not conquer Jebusites living in Jerusalem. The Jebusites live with the people of Benjamine in Jerusalem to this very day.
>
> **1:27** But the men of Manasseh did not conquer Beth Shan, Taanach, or their surrounding towns. Nor did they conquer the people

living in Dor, Ibleam, Megiddo or their surrounding towns. The Canaanites managed to remain in those areas.

1:29 The men of Ephraim did not conquer the Canaanites living in Gezer. The Canaanites lived among them in Gezer. **30** The men of Zebulun did not conquer the people living in Kitron or Nahalol. The Canaanites lived among them and were forced to do hard labor. **31** The men of Asher did not conquer the people living in Acco or Sidon. Nor did they conquer or Ahlab, Aczib, Helbah, Aphek, or Rehob. **32** The people of Asher lived among the Canaanites residing in the land because they did not conquer them. **33** The men of Naphtali did not conquer the people living in Beth Shemesh or Beth Anath. The Canaanites living in Beth Shemesh and Beth Anath were forced to do hard labor for them.

Which of the twelve tribes obeyed God's command?

---

3. The Cycle of Judges

A. Re-read 2:6–23. Note especially verses 7, 11, 14, 16. In each of these verses, what is the relationship of the nation's people to God? We will see this cycle again and again in Judges.

worship

did evil

Lord furious - handed over to enemies

raised up leader/ delivered from enemies

B. Note how the cycle is seen in other portions of Scripture. Read Psalm 106:34–39.

Psalm 106:34 They did not destroy the nations
as the LORD had commanded them to do,

106:35 They mixed in with the nations
and learned their ways.

106:36 They worshiped their idols,
which became a snare to them.

106:37 They sacrificed their sons
and daughters to demons.

106:38 They shed innocent blood—
the blood of their sons and daughters,
whom they sacrificed to the idols of Canaan. The land was pol-
luted by bloodshed.

106:39 They were defiled by their deeds,
and unfaithful in their actions.

What is the people's response to God's commands?

_____

_____

_____

_____

C. Read Psalm 106:40–43.

106:40 So the Lord was angry with his people
and despised the people who belonged to him.

106:41 He handed them over to the nations,
and those who hated them ruled over them.

106:42 Their enemies oppressed them;
they were subject to their authority.

106:43 Many times he delivered them,
but they had a rebellious attitude
and degraded themselves by their sin.

What is God's response?

_____

_____

_____

_____

D. Read Psalm 106:44–45.

> **106:44** Yet he took notice of their distress
> when he heard their cry for help,
> **106:45** He remembered his covenant with them,
> and relented because of his great loyal love.

What is God's response?

_____

_____

_____

_____

Right at the beginning of the Book of Judges we see the pattern of sin, distress, crying to God, and deliverance set forth. (Some have alliterated this cycle: sin, suffering or servitude, supplication, and salvation.) Then the book seems to follow a pattern of showing us how this cycle repeats itself.

4. Think of a time in your life when you've seen the cycle of sin, suffering or servitude, supplication, and salvation. Which best describes where you are right now? Is there something you can do to improve where you are? If so, what?

_____

_____

_____

_____

5. Baal was the rain and fertility god of the Canaanites, the people who inhabited the land the Israelites were to conquer. The Ashtars were local manifestations of the goddess Astarte, the female counterpart to Baal. The worship of these false gods included animal sacrifice, male and female prostitution, and even human sacrifice. With that in mind, read Judges 2:2, 12–13.

Judges 2:2 but you must not make an agreement with the people who live in this land. You should tear down the altars where they worship. But you have disobeyed me. Why would you do such a thing?

2:12 They abandoned the Lord God of their ancestors who had brought them out of the land of Egypt. They followed other gods— the gods of the nations who lived around them. They worshiped them and made the Lord angry. **2:13** They abandoned the Lord and worshiped Baal and the Ashtars.

What sins did the people commit?

_____

_____

_____

WEDNESDAY: OTHNIEL—HE CAME, HE SAW, HE CONQUERED.

1. Read Judges 1:14–15.

1:14 One time Acsah [Caleb's daughter] came and charmed her father so she could ask him for some land. When she got down from her donkey, Caleb said to her, "What would you like?" **1:15** She answered, "Please give me a special present. Since you have given me land in the Negev, now give me springs of water." So Caleb gave her both the upper and lower springs.

At the time of the judges, water symbolized fertility. Then, as now, it was essential to survival. We who live in homes with several faucets may quickly forget how important it would be to have water available on one's land.

How would you describe Caleb's relationship with his daughter based on what you just read?

_____

_____

_____

_____

2. Caleb was not only a great leader in the nation but also made life as secure as possible for his daughter. If you have children, what are some ways in which you can follow his example this week?

_____

_____

_____

3. Read Judges 1:12–15 and Joshua 15:13–19 below.

Judges 1:12 Caleb said, "To the man who attacks and captures Kiriath Sepher I will give my daughter Acsah as a wife." **1:13** When Othniel son of Kenaz, Caleb's younger brother, captured it, Caleb gave him his daughter Acsah as a wife. **1:14** One time Acsah came and charmed her father so she could ask him for some land. When she got down from her donkey, Caleb said to her, "What would you like?" **1:15** She answered, "Please give me a special present. Since you have given me land in the Negev, now give me springs of water." So Caleb gave her both the upper and lower springs.

Joshua 15:13 Caleb son of Jephunneh was assigned Kiriath Arba (that is Hebron) within the tribe of Judah, according to the Lord's instructions to Joshua. (Arba was the father of Anak.) **15:14** Caleb drove out from there three Anakites—Sheshai, Ahiman, and Talmai, descendants of Anak. **15:15** From there he attacked the people of Debir. (Debir used to be called Kiriath Sepher.) **15:16** Caleb said, "To the man who attacks and captures Kiriath Sepher I will give my daughter Acsah as a wife." **15:17** When Othniel son of Kenaz, Caleb's brother, captured it, Caleb gave Acsah his daughter to him as a wife.

15:18 One time Acsah came and charmed her father so she could ask him for some land. When she got down from her donkey, Caleb said to her, "What would you like?" **15:19** She answered, "Please give me a special present. Since you have given me land in the Negev, now give me springs of water. So he gave her both upper and lower springs.

Summarize Othniel's background.

_____

_____

_____

_____

4. Read Judges 3:7–11. Othniel appears as the first judge and as a model of what a judge should be:

> **3:7** The Israelites did evil in the Lord's sight. They forgot the Lord their God and worshiped the Baals and the Asherahs. **3:8** The Lord was furious with Israel and turned them over to King Cushan-Rishathaim of Aram-Naharaim. They were Cushan-Rishathaim's subjects for eight years. **3:9** When the Israelites cried out for help to the Lord, he raised up a deliverer for the Israelites who rescued them. His name was Othniel son of Kenaz, Caleb's younger brother. **3:10** The Lord's spirit empowered him and he led Israel. When he went to do battle, the Lord handed over to him King Cushan-Rishathaim of Aram and he overpowered him. **3:11** The land had rest for forty years; then Othniel son of Kenaz died.

> *Cushan-Rishathaim cannot be further identified, but the latter part of the name "Rishathaim" means "double wickedness."*
> —Eugene Merrill,
> Kingdom of Priests

5. What does Judges 3:7 say has happened to Israel?

_____

_____

_____

_____

_____

6. What does Othniel do, and what are the results (vv. 9–11)?

_____

_____

 ## THURSDAY: ICE-VEINED EHUD

1. Ehud, a Benjamite, is the next judge. The oppression that occurs during his time appears to be localized near Jericho ("The City of Palms," Judg. 3:13).

Some scholars believe a group of Benjamite warriors bound their right hands so they could learn to fight both right- and left-handed. Highlight references to left-handedness in the verses below:

Judges 3:15 When the Israelites cried out for help to the Lord, and raised up a deliverer for them. His name was Ehud son of Gera the Benjamite, a left-handed man. The Israelites sent him to King Eglon of Moab with their tribute payment.

Judges 20:16 Among this army were seven hundred specially-trained left-handed soldiers from Gibeah. Each one could sling a stone and hit even the smallest target.

In Judges 3:15 we read that Eglon was king of Moab. If you've ever studied the Book of Ruth, you know Ruth was a Moabitess. Moabites were descendants of Lot and his incestuous daughters (see Gen. 19:35–37), and they worshiped a god named Chemosh, to whom they sometimes sacrificed their firstborn children.

1 Chronicles 12:2 They were armed with bows and could shoot arrows or sling stones right or left-handed. They were fellow tribesmen of Saul from Benjamin).

Re-read Judges 3:12–30.

3:12 The Israelites again did evil in the Lord's sight. The Lord gave King Eglon of Moab control over Israel because they had done evil in the Lord's sight. **3:13** Eglon allied with the Ammonites and Amalekites. He came and defeated Israel, and they seized the City of Date Palm Trees. **3:14** The Israelites were subject to King Eglon of Moab for eighteen years.

3:15 When the Israelites cried out for help to the Lord, he raised up a deliverer for them. His name was Ehud son of Gera the

Benjaminite, a left-handed man. The Israelites sent him to King Eglon of Moab with their tribute payment. **3:16** Ehud made himself a sword—it had two edges and was eighteen inches long. He strapped it under his coat on his right thigh. **3:17** He brought the tribute payment to King Eglon of Moab. (Now Eglon was a very fat man.)

3:18 After Ehud brought the tribute payment, he dismissed the people who had carried it. **3:19** But he went back once he reached the carved images at Gilgal. He said to Eglon, "I have a secret message for you, O king." Eglon said, "Be quiet!" All his attendants left. **3:20** When Ehud approached him, he was sitting in his well-ventilated upper room all by himself. Ehud said, "I have a divine message for you." When Eglon rose up from his seat, **3:21** Ehud reached with his left hand, pulled the sword from his right thigh, and drove it into Eglon's belly. **3:22** The handle went in after the blade, and the fat closed around the blade, for Ehud did not pull the sword out of his belly. **3:23** As Ehud went out into the vestibule, he closed the doors of the upper room behind him and locked them.

3:24 When Ehud had left, Eglon's servants came and saw the locked doors of the upper room. They said, "He must be relieving himself in the well-ventilated inner room." **3:25** They waited so long they were embarrassed, but he still did not open the doors of the upper room. Finally they took the key and opened the doors. Right before their eyes was their master, sprawled out dead on the floor! **3:26** Now Ehud had escaped while they were delaying. When he passed the carved images, he escaped to Seirah.

3:27 When he reached Seirah, he blew a trumpet in the Ephraimite hill country. The Israelites went down with him from the hill country, with Ehud in the lead. **3:28** He said to them, "Follow me, for the Lord is about to defeat your enemies, the Moabites!" They followed him, captured the fords of the Jordan River opposite Moab, and did not let anyone cross. **3:29** That day they killed about ten thousand Moabites—all strong, capable warriors; not one escaped. **3:30** Israel humiliated Moab that day, and the land had rest for eighty years.

2. Summarize: what did Ehud do, and what were the results?

_____

_____

_____

3. Ehud demonstrated his faith by killing an evil king. Today we are not called to literally kill in the name of righteousness. Instead, both Jesus and Paul tell us to love our enemies (Matt. 5:44; Rom. 12:14). The Son's kingdom is not a kingdom brought about by violence (Matt. 26:52). Yet God does call us to engage in spiritual warfare (Eph. 6:11), to take drastic action to eradicate evil from our lives (Matt. 5:30), and to help remove it from others' lives (Matt. 18:15). Is there anything you sense God leading you to do to take drastic action against evil? If so, what? Pray for divine enablement to do what you need to do.

FRIDAY: SHAMGAR THE CREATIVE

1. Read Judges 3:31; 5:6.

> **Judges 3:31** After Ehud came Shamgar son of Anath; he killed six hundred Philistines with an oxgoad and, like Ehud, delivered Israel.
>
> **Judges 5:6** In the days of Shamgar son of Anath, in the days of Jael caravans disappeared; travelers had to go on winding side roads.

We don't know much about Shamgar, but what do we learn from these verses?

- Shamgar's name has four consonants in Hebrew, whereas most have only three. Was he a foreigner? His name could also be translated "son of Anath," which is the name for a Canaanite goddess.
- What does Judges 5:6 mean? It would appear that Israel's Canaanite enemies controlled the highways, and thus the Israelites had to find alternate routes.

2. What does Shamgar's use of an ox goad to kill so many Philistines tell us about him?

_____

_____

_____

_____

3. Why was killing Philistines such a good thing?

An ox goad was used for goading oxen. It's a long stick with a pointed end used for prodding animals, especially useful if you don't want to get too close. An agricultural tool, it was probably eight to ten feet long. At one end was probably an iron spear and at the other a piece of the same metal, only flattened. This is a pretty unconventional weapon.

Joshua 13:1 When Joshua was very old, the Lord told him, "You are very old, and a great deal of land remains to be conquered. **13:2** "This is the land that remains: all the territories of the Philistines and all the Geshurites. . . ."

_____

_____

The Philistines were an uncircumcised people inhabiting southwestern Palestine. The name "Palestine" itself refers to their country. They are noted 286 times in the Old Testament, and their country is mentioned eight times. In Genesis 10:14 (see also 1 Chr. 1:12) they're reckoned with other tribes in Mizraim (Egypt) as descendants of Ham and as cousins of the old inhabitants of Babylonia (Gen. 10:6). According to the Old Testament and monuments alike, the Philistines were a Semitic people who worshiped two Babylonian deities, Dagon (see 1 Sam. 5:2) and the Ashtoreths (see 1 Sam. 31:10), both of whom were adored very early in Babylonia.[2]

SATURDAY: EXTREME WARFARE

I've often said that the Book of Judges was written especially with junior high boys in mind. I mean, if it weren't in the Bible, their parents wouldn't let them read it.

[2] *International Standard Bible Encyclopedia,* "Philistine." www.bible.org/ISBE.

Think about it. There's Ehud the Hero stabbing the fat king of Moab so his guts fall out, while all the servants think the king is taking a *really* long time on the john. Eew!

And we have Jael, the She-Hero, enticing Sisera with a nice bowl of milk, sending him off to sleep like a fat cat—only to nail him to the floor with a tent peg through the head. Shuzzam!

Then there's Shamgar-the-Creative. I mean, stabbing to death six hundred Philistines—with an ox goad?

And all this to the glory of God?

Ahem, I say.

And all the junior high boys cry out, "Cool! Tell me another Bible story!"

But what about those of us raised on *Little House on the Prairie* and *Pollyanna*?

Often we expect a G-rated God only to discover to our surprise (and sometimes our disappointment) that His story is more like a fast-paced R-rated movie than the super-edited G-rated TV. Consider how many people were shocked at the "R" rating and the violence in *The Passion of the Christ.* Yet the Bible scholar I sat next to as I watched it told me the actual events were probably much bloodier than that. And honestly, do we really want to tone down the drama illustrating how far God would go to show His love? It's not at all the same thing as gratuitous violence.

Consider the following.

One evening last weekend as I drove home from a conference through a mist of light rain, I found myself sitting on the eastbound lane of a highway that looked more like a parking lot than a passable road. Pretty soon I heard sirens, and then I knew the reason for the backup—an accident ahead. I noticed that none of the four lanes headed westbound toward me had any cars in them at all.

Vehicles on my side of the highway inched forward bit by bit, and pretty soon it all came into view—three police cars, two ambulances, and a smashed red van with noise overhead. I looked up to spot a helicopter and then watched open-mouthed as the pilot dodged electrical wires and landed squarely in the center of an eastbound lane.

So the wreck was on the other side from where I was, with all four lanes shut down in preparation for the aircraft's arrival. And my own side was slowed only by gawking onlookers.

Now who would want to gawk at that?

Well, frankly, I confess that I looked, too. I prayed the people would be OK. I prayed I would see nothing dramatic. But I still looked.

So what's that about? Much as we want to look away, we want to see the action. We're drawn to life and death. We're compelled by the drama. And God is in the drama.

When God's people entered the Promised Land, He wanted the place cleaned out before His people got defiled by the sick practices of those who lived there. And while today we're not to physically hurt someone to further God's kingdom, we're still to engage in warfare—serious warfare. Take a look at some verses from Mark 9:

"If your hand causes you to sin, cut it off!" (v. 43).

"If your foot causes you to sin, cut it off!" (v. 45).

"If your eye causes you to sin, tear it out!" (v. 47).

Extreme obedience.

God hates sin. While the enemies of His people may have transitioned from physical to spiritual in God's unfolding plan, the underlying truth remains—God hates, hates, hates sin. *Hates* it.

The apostle Paul exhorts us to "hate what is evil; cling to what is good." He is not calling us to hate people. (Remember that Jesus also told us to love even our enemies.) Rather, through the use of hyperbole, God is letting us know how much He wants us to hate self-centered living, unkindness, evil.

With that in mind, how much are you willing to hate for the glory of God?

Prayer: *O Father, have mercy on me, a sinner. Thank You for sending Your Son, Jesus, the perfect sacrifice whose payment was sufficient to make amends for all I've done to offend You. I believe in Him through Your grace and enabling. Forgive my incomplete obedience, for my tolerance of things in my life that You loathe. Give me a heart to abhor what is evil and to cling to what is good. Help me to love people fiercely and to hate evil courageously. Thank You that even when I've sinned, I can turn to You and find that You continually have compassion. In the name of Your sinless Son I pray. Amen.*

For Memorization: "When the Lord raised up leaders for them, the Lord was with each leader and delivered the people from their enemies while the leader remained alive. The Lord felt sorry for them when they cried out in agony because of what their harsh oppressors did to them." (Judg. 2:18)

WEEK 2 OF 6

The Good and the Reluctant: Judges 4—5

Scripture: "May all your enemies perish like this, O Lord! But may those who love you shine like the rising sun at its brightest." (Judges 5:31)

After attending a lecture at the seminary where I teach, I saw a female student whom I had not seen in months. After greeting me, she enthusiastically told me about the exciting ministries God was allowing in and through her life. Then she concluded with a puzzling statement: "It's just sad to think that God is having to use me because a man somewhere has failed."

"Excuse me?" I was pretty sure I must have misunderstood.

"God wanted a godly man to lead, but since he apparently didn't, I get to be part of 'Plan B.' I'm glad for God to use me, but it makes me feel bad that someone failed." I heard a marked sadness in her voice.

I asked where she got that idea, and she said it was right out of the book of Judges—Deborah's story, in fact. Someone had taught her

22

that a godly woman leading meant a man had failed somewhere. "God uses a good woman only when a good man can't be found," she said.

We talked further, and she explained more, pointing out that Barak was supposed to be the judge but that when he turned out to be a wimp, God raised up Deborah.

"What makes you think Barak was supposed to be the judge—that he was 'Plan A'?" I asked, noting that Barak doesn't come into the picture until Deborah is already well established as a leader and a prophetess. In fact, Deborah summons Barak and speaks God's word to him before we know what Barak is going to do.

"But God knew ahead of time what Barak's response would be. And we know God would prefer to use a man to lead instead of a woman."

"How do we know that?"

"The story of Deborah."

Circular reasoning.

I shook my head. Obviously continuing to discuss Deborah's story wasn't going to help. So we considered another prophetess in the Bible. We find her story in 2 Kings 22:14–20:

> **2 Kings 22:14** So Hilkiah the priest, Ahikam, Acbor, Shaphan, and Asaiah went to Huldah the prophetess, the wife of Shullam son of Tikvah, the son of Harhas, the supervisor of the wardrobe. (She lived in Jerusalem in the Mishneh district.) They stated their business, **22:15** and she said to them: "This is what the Lord God of Israel says: 'Say this to the man who sent you to me: **22:16** "This is what the Lord says: 'I am about to bring disaster on this place and its residents, the details of which are recorded on the scroll which the king of Judah has read. **22:17** This will happen because they have abandoned me and offered sacrifices to other gods, angering me with all the idols they have made. My anger will ignite against this place and will not be extinguished.'" **22:18** Say this to the king of Judah, who sent you to seek an oracle from the Lord: "This is what the Lord God of Israel says concerning the words you have heard: **22:19** 'You displayed a sensitive spirit and humbled yourself before the Lord when you heard how I intended to make this place and its residents into an appalling example of an accursed people. You tore your clothes and wept before me, and I have heard you,' says the Lord. **22:20** 'Therefore I will allow you to die and be buried in peace. You will not have to witness all the disaster I will bring on this place.'" "" Then they reported back to the king.

Huldah. The name sounds as if she were built like a linebacker, weighing in at more than two hundred pounds, taking garbage off no one, doesn't it? Who knows? Perhaps she was actually quite feminine. At any rate, the first person mentioned in the list of those who consulted with Huldah was Hilkiah the priest (2 Kgs. 22:14). Interestingly, we find him mentioned in the Book of Jeremiah, which begins with these words: "The following is a record of what Jeremiah *son of Hilkiah* prophesied and did. He was one of the priests who lived at Anathoth in the territory of the tribe of Benjamin" (Jer. 1:1, emphasis added). In other words, one of the very men who sought God's word from Huldah was the father of Jeremiah, the prophet (2 Chr. 35:25). But there's more—the prophets Zephaniah (Zeph. 1:1), probably Nahum, and Habakkuk were also living at the time and were even presumably in the same city—Jerusalem!

Are we to conclude that all these men were spiritual wimps? Isn't it more logical to conclude that God sometimes uses a good woman even when a good man *can* be found?

Consider the many female leaders and prophets in Scripture starting with Miriam (Mic. 6:4)—she led during the time of *Moses.* And there's Deborah (Judg. 4) and Huldah (2 Kgs. 22) in the Old Testament. In the New Testament we find Anna (Luke 2:36) and Philip's daughters (Acts 21:9) and the young female prophets (Acts 2:17). This is far from being an exhaustive list.

Apparently God sometimes decides to use a woman as the Plan A, first-best, nobody-failed option.

Are you willing and ready to be that woman?

MONDAY: BACKGROUND

1. Prayerfully read Judges 4—5.

Judges 4

4:1 The Israelites again did evil in the Lord's sight after Ehud's death. **4:2** The Lord turned them over to King Jabin of Canaan, who ruled in Hazor. The general of his army was Sisera, who lived in Harosheth Haggoyim. **4:3** The Israelites cried out for help to the Lord, for Sisera had nine hundred chariots with iron-rimmed wheels, and he cruelly oppressed the Israelites for twenty years.

4:4 Now Deborah, a prophetess, wife of Lappidoth, was leading Israel at that time. **4:5** She would sit under the Date Palm Tree of Deborah between Ramah and Bethel in the Ephraimite hill country. The Israelites would come up to her to have their disputes settled.

4:6 She summoned Barak son of Abinoam from Kedesh in Naphtali. She said to him, "Is it not true that the Lord God of Israel is commanding you? Go, march to Mount Tabor! Take with you ten thousand men from Naphtali and Zebulun! **4:7** I will bring Sisera, the general of Jabin's army, to you at the Kishon River, along with his chariots and huge army. I will hand him over to you." **4:8** Barak said to her, "If you go with me, I will go. But if you do not go with me, I will not go." **4:9** She said, "I will indeed go with you. But you will not gain fame on the expedition you are taking, for the Lord will turn Sisera over to a woman." Deborah got up and went with Barak to Kedesh. **4:10** Barak summoned men from Zebulun and Naphtali to Kedesh. Ten thousand men followed him; Deborah went up with him as well. **4:11** Now Heber the Kenite had moved away from the Kenites, the descendants of Hobab, Moses' father-in-law. He lived near the tree in Zaanannim near Kedesh.

4:12 When Sisera heard that Barak son of Abinoam had gone up to Mount Tabor, **4:13** he ordered all his chariotry—nine hundred chariots with iron-rimmed wheels—and all the troops he had with him to go from Harosheth-Haggoyim to the River Kishon. **4:14** Deborah said to Barak, "Spring into action, for this is the day the Lord is handing Sisera over to you! Has the Lord not taken the lead?" Barak quickly went down from Mount Tabor with ten thousand men following him. **4:15** The Lord routed Sisera, all his chariotry, and all his army with the edge of the sword. Sisera jumped out of his chariot and ran away on foot. **4:16** Now Barak chased the chariots and the army all the way to Harosheth Haggoyim. Sisera's whole army died by the edge of the sword; not even one survived.

4:17 Now Sisera ran away on foot to the tent of Jael, wife of Heber the Kenite, for King Jabin of Hazor and the family of Heber the Kenite had made a peace treaty. **34:18** Jael came out to welcome Sisera. She said to him, "Stop and rest, my lord. Stop and rest with me. Don't be afraid." So Sisera stopped to rest in her tent, and she put a blanket over him. **4:19** He said to her, "Give me a little water to drink, because I'm thirsty." She opened a goatskin container of milk and gave him some milk to drink. Then she covered him up again. **4:20** He said to her, "Stand watch at the entrance to the tent. If anyone comes along and asks you, 'Is there a man here?' say 'No.'" **4:21** Then Jael wife of Heber took a tent peg in one hand and a hammer in the other.

She crept up on him, drove the tent peg through his temple into the ground while he was asleep from exhaustion, and he died. **4:22** Now Barak was chasing Sisera. Jael went out to welcome him. She said to him, "Come here and I will show you the man you are searching for." He went with her into the tent, and there he saw Sisera sprawled out dead with the tent peg in his temple.

4:23 That day God humiliated King Jabin of Canaan, before the Israelites. **4:24** Israel's power continued to overwhelm King Jabin of Canaan until they did away with him.

Judges 5

5:1 On that day Deborah and Barak son of Abinoam sang this victory song:

5:2 "When the leaders took the lead in Israel, When the people answered the call to war—Praise the Lord!

5:3 Hear, O kings! Pay attention, O rulers! I will sing to the Lord! I will sing to the Lord God of Israel!

5:4 O Lord, when you departed from Seir, when you marched from Edom's plains, the earth shook, the heavens poured down, the clouds poured down rain.

5:5 The mountains trembled before the Lord, the God of Sinai; before the Lord God of Israel.

5:6 In the days of Shamgar son of Anath, in the days of Jael caravans disappeared; travelers had to go on winding side roads.

5:7 Warriors were scarce, they were scarce in Israel, until you arose, Deborah, until you arose as a motherly protector in Israel.

5:8 God chose new leaders, then fighters appeared in the city gates; but, I swear, not a shield or spear could be found, among forty military units in Israel.

5:9 My heart went out to Israel's leaders, to the people who answered the call to war. Praise the Lord!

5:10 You who ride on light-colored female donkeys, who sit on saddle cloths, you who walk on the road, pay attention!

5:11 Hear the sound of those who divide the sheep among the watering places; there they tell of the Lord's victorious deeds, the victorious deeds of his warriors in Israel. Then the Lord's people went down to the city gates—

5:12 Wake up, wake up, Deborah! Wake up, wake up, sing a song! Get up, Barak! Capture your prisoners of war, son of Abinoam!

5:13 Then the survivors came down to the mighty ones; the Lord's people came down to me as warriors.

5:14 They came from Ephraim, who uprooted Amalek, they follow after you, Benjamin, with your soldiers. From Makir leaders came down, from Zebulun came the ones who march carrying an officer's staff.

5:15 Issachar's leaders were with Deborah, the men of Issachar supported Barak, into the valley they were sent under Barak's command. Among the clans of Reuben there was intense heart searching.

5:16 Why do you remain among the sheepfolds, listening to the shepherds playing their pipes for their flocks? As for the clans of Reuben—there was intense heart searching.

5:17 Gilead stayed put beyond the Jordan River. As for Dan—why did he seek temporary employment in the shipyards? Asher remained on the seacoast, he stayed put by his harbors.

5:18 The men of Zebulun were not concerned about their lives; Naphtali charged on to the battlefields.

5:19 Kings came, they fought; the kings of Canaan fought, at Taanach by the waters of Megiddo, but they took no silver as plunder.

5:20 From the sky the stars fought, from their paths in the heavens they fought against Sisera.

5:21 The Kishon River carried them off; the river confronted them—the Kishon River. Step on the necks of the strong!

5:22 The horses' hooves pounded the ground; the stallions galloped madly.

5:23 'Call judgment down on Meroz', says the Lord's angelic messenger; 'Be sure to call judgment down on those who live there, because they did not come to help in the Lord's battle, to help in the Lord's battle against the warriors.'

5:24 The most rewarded of women should be Jael, the wife of Heber the Kenite! She should be the most rewarded of women who live in tents.

5:25 He asked for water, and she gave him milk; in a bowl fit for important men, she served him curds.

5:26 Her left hand reached for the tent peg, her right hand for the workmen's hammer. She "hammered" Sisera, she shattered his skull, she smashed his head, she drove the tent peg through his temple.

5:27 Between her feet he collapsed, he fell limp and was lifeless; between her feet he collapsed and fell limp, in the spot where he collapsed, there he fell limp—violently murdered!

5:28 Through the window she looked; Sisera's mother cried out through the lattice: 'Why is his chariot so slow to return? Why are the hoofbeats of his chariot-horses delayed?'

5:29 The wisest of her ladies answer; indeed she even thinks to herself,

5:30 'No doubt they are gathering and dividing the plunder—a girl or two for each man to rape! Sisera is grabbing up colorful cloth, he is grabbing up colorful embroidered cloth, two pieces of colorful embroidered cloth, for the neck of the plunderer!'

5:31 May all your enemies perish like this, O Lord! But may those who love you shine like the rising sun at its brightest!" And the land had rest for forty years.

2. Note anything that speaks to you or that you find interesting.

_____

_____

_____

_____

_____

3. What questions do you have?

_____

_____

_____

_____

_____

1. Read Judges 4:4–5.

> **4:4** Now Deborah, a prophetess, the wife of Lappidoth, was leading Israel at that time. **5** She would sit under the Date Palm Tree of Deborah between Ramah and Bethel in the Ephraimite hill country. The Israelites would come up to her to have their disputes settled.

What do we learn about Deborah?

_____

_____

_____

2. Note that Deborah was a prophetess. What does she tell Barak? (4:6–7.)

> **4:6** She summoned Barak son of Abinoam from Kedesh in Naphtali. She said to him, "Is it not true that the Lord God of Israel is commanding you? Go, march to Mount Tabor! Take with you ten thousand men from Naphtali and Zebulun!
>
> **4:7** I will bring Sisera, the general of Jabin's army, to you at the Kishon River, along with his chariots and huge army. I will hand him over to you."

_____

_____

_____

_____

3. Read Barak's response to the Lord's command (4:8):

> **Judges 4:8** Barak said to her, "If you go with me, I will go. But if you do not go with me, I will not go."

What do you think of his response? What do you suppose God thought of it?

_____

_____

_____

4. Barak had faith, but with hesitancy. In response to God's command, he said, "I'll obey if . . ." What commands from the Lord are you hesitant in applying?

_____

_____

_____

5. Is there an area of your life in which you're outlining conditions God must meet before you'll obey? If so, what? Spend some time praying about them.

_____

_____

_____

_____

6. Deborah didn't abandon Barak for his lack of faith. Rather, she accompanied him and gave him strength in accomplishing God's purpose. Is there someone in your life whose faith you can bolster by your presence? If so, who is it, and what can you do?

_____

_____

1. Read Judges 4:11, 17 (below) to become familiar with Jael. Note that she was living in enemy territory.

> **Judges 4:11** Now Heber the Kenite had moved away from the Kenites, the descendants of Hobab, Moses' father-in-law. He lived near the tree in Zaanannim near Kedesh.

> **4:17** Now Sisera ran away on foot to the tent of Jael, wife of Heber the Kenite, for King Jabin of Hazor and the family of Heber the Kenite had made a peace treaty.

2. Read Judges 4:16–22 below. Note that a tent peg would have been readily accessible, as it was a woman's job to pitch the tent in Jael's day.

> **4:16** Now Barak chased the chariots and the army all the way to Harosheth Haggoyim. Sisera's whole army died by the edge of the sword; not even one survived.

> **4:17** Now Sisera ran away on foot to the tent of Jael, wife of Heber the Kenite, for King Jabin of Hazor and the family of Heber the Kenite had made a peace treaty. **4:18** Jael came out to welcome Sisera. She said to him, "Stop and rest, my lord. Stop and rest with me. Don't be afraid." So Sisera stopped to rest in her tent, and she put a blanket over him. **4:19** He said to her, "Give me a little water to drink, because I'm thirsty." She opened a goatskin container of milk and gave him some milk to drink. Then she covered him up again. **4:20** He said to her, "Stand watch at the entrance to the tent. If anyone comes along and asks you, 'Is there a man here?' say 'No.' " **4:21** Then Jael wife of Heber took a tent peg in one hand and a hammer in the other. She crept up on him, drove the tent peg through his temple into the ground while he was asleep from exhaustion, and he died. **4:22** Now Barak was chasing Sisera. Jael went out to welcome him. She said to him, "Come here and I will show you the man you are searching for." He went with her into the tent, and there he saw Sisera sprawled out dead with the tent peg in his temple.

How is Jael's cunning similar to that of Ehud's (Judges 3:12–30, which we looked at last week)?

_____

_____

_____

_____

_____

3. Jael used an unconventional tool, a tent peg, to accomplish God's purpose. Shamgar used an ox goad. These people used what they had and were familiar with to glorify God. Is there something in your life that's unconventional but that you can use to glorify God? If so, what is it, and how might you use it?

_____

_____

_____

_____

_____

4. Jael engages in *physical* warfare to the glory of God. In Ephesians 6:13 we read that the apostle Paul encouraged every believer to engage in *spiritual* warfare. What battles are you fighting? Spend some time praying for God to give you victory and to glorify himself through your circumstances.

You've heard of Paul Revere, right? He was an eighteenth-century American patriot who carried news to Lexington, Massachusetts, of the British army's approach at the start of the Revolutionary War. That's a short prose description of what he did. The poetry version by Henry Wadsworth Longfellow begins like this:

Listen, my children, and you shall hear
Of the midnight ride of Paul Revere,
On the eighteenth of April, in Seventy-five;
Hardly a man is now alive
Who remembers that famous day and year.

We have something similar here in Judges. First there's a prose account of a great historical event; then we have a parallel poetic account.

Really? A good woman warrior in the Old Testament? Women called to engage in warfare in the New Testament? Interestingly enough, the Hebrew terms used in Proverbs 31 to describe the ideal "woman of valor" are full of warrior imagery.

1. Read Judges 5.

Judges 5

5:1 On that day Deborah and Barak son of Abinoam sang this victory song:

5:2 "When the leaders took the lead in Israel, When the people answered the call to war—Praise the Lord!

5:3 Hear, O kings! Pay attention, O rulers! I will sing to the Lord! I will sing to the Lord God of Israel!

5:4 O Lord, when you departed from Seir, when you marched from Edom's plains, the earth shook, the heavens poured down, the clouds poured down rain.

5:5 The mountains trembled before the Lord, the God of Sinai; before the Lord God of Israel.

5:6 In the days of Shamgar son of Anath, in the days of Jael caravans disappeared; travelers had to go on winding side roads.

5:7 Warriors were scarce, they were scarce in Israel, until you arose, Deborah, until you arose as a motherly protector in Israel.

5:8 God chose new leaders, then fighters appeared in the city gates; but, I swear, not a shield or spear could be found, among forty military units in Israel.

5:9 My heart went out to Israel's leaders, to the people who answered the call to war. Praise the Lord!

5:10 You who ride on light-colored female donkeys, who sit on saddle cloths, you who walk on the road, pay attention!

5:11 Hear the sound of those who divide the sheep among the watering places; there they tell of the Lord's victorious deeds, the victorious deeds of his warriors in Israel. Then the Lord's people went down to the city gates—

5:12 Wake up, wake up, Deborah! Wake up, wake up, sing a song! Get up, Barak! Capture your prisoners of war, son of Abinoam!

5:13 Then the survivors came down to the mighty ones; the Lord's people came down to me as warriors.

5:14 They came from Ephraim, who uprooted Amalek, they follow after you, Benjamin, with your soldiers. From Makir leaders came down, from Zebulun came the ones who march carrying an officer's staff.

5:15 Issachar's leaders were with Deborah, the men of Issachar supported Barak, into the valley they were sent under Barak's command. Among the clans of Reuben there was intense heart searching.

5:16 Why do you remain among the sheepfolds, listening to the shepherds playing their pipes for their flocks? As for the clans of Reuben—there was intense heart searching.

5:17 Gilead stayed put beyond the Jordan River. As for Dan— why did he seek temporary employment in the shipyards? Asher remained on the seacoast, he stayed put by his harbors.

5:18 The men of Zebulun were not concerned about their lives; Naphtali charged on to the battlefields.

5:19 Kings came, they fought; the kings of Canaan fought, at Taanach by the waters of Megiddo, but they took no silver as plunder.

5:20 From the sky the stars fought, from their paths in the heavens they fought against Sisera.

5:21 The Kishon River carried them off; the river confronted them—the Kishon River. Step on the necks of the strong!

5:22 The horses' hooves pounded the ground; the stallions galloped madly.

5:23 'Call judgment down on Meroz', says the Lord's angelic messenger; 'Be sure to call judgment down on those who live there, because they did not come to help in the Lord's battle, to help in the Lord's battle against the warriors.'

5:24 The most rewarded of women should be Jael, the wife of Heber the Kenite! She should be the most rewarded of women who live in tents.

5:25 He asked for water, and she gave him milk; in a bowl fit for important men, she served him curds.

5:26 Her left hand reached for the tent peg, her right hand for the workmen's hammer. She "hammered" Sisera, she shattered his skull, she smashed his head, she drove the tent peg through his temple.

5:27 Between her feet he collapsed, he fell limp and was lifeless; between her feet he collapsed and fell limp, in the spot where he collapsed, there he fell limp—violently murdered!

5:28 Through the window she looked; Sisera's mother cried out through the lattice: 'Why is his chariot so slow to return? Why are the hoofbeats of his chariot-horses delayed?'

5:29 The wisest of her ladies answer; indeed she even thinks to herself,

5:30 'No doubt they are gathering and dividing the plunder—a girl or two for each man to rape! Sisera is grabbing up colorful cloth, he is grabbing up colorful embroidered cloth, two pieces of colorful embroidered cloth, for the neck of the plunderer!'

5:31 May all your enemies perish like this, O Lord! But may those who love you shine like the rising sun at its brightest!" And the land had rest for forty years.

2. Notice how the story is retold. How does chapter 4 differ from chapter 5 in terms of writing style?

_____

_____

_____

_____

_____

3. Notice how Sisera's mother is described in the poetic account (5:28–30). According to the text, where did Sisera lay dead? (Go back to vv. 24–27.)

_____

_____

_____

A. What does Sisera's mother's maid propose as the possible cause for Sisera's delay? (5:30.)

_____

_____

_____

B. In the Hebrew, Judges 5:30 is worded coarsely: "A womb, two wombs for every warrior." This suggests that Sisera's mother envisions her son and his army out raping Hebrew women. What irony do you see when comparing verses 5:27 and 5:30?

_____

_____

_____

_____

C. What is the expected spiritual response to this entire story (v. 31)?

_____

_____

_____

4. Consider 4:15; 5:20. What do these verses tell you about God's involvement in helping His people accomplish His will?

> **4:15** The Lord routed Sisera, all his chariotry, and all his army with the edge of the sword. Sisera jumped out of his chariot and ran away on foot. **5:20** From the sky the stars fought, from their paths in the heavens they fought against Sisera.

_____

_____

_____

5. In Barak's day it pleased God for the Israelite army to fight. Consider God's will for your life today. We know He wants you to be thankful, to be holy, to have the fruit of the Spirit. Ask for His help in accomplishing what would please Him in your life.

FRIDAY: DEBORAH THE LEADER

1. Read Judges 4:14–16.

> **4:14** Deborah said to Barak, "Spring into action, for this is the day the Lord is handing Sisera over to you! Has the Lord not taken the lead?" Barak quickly went down from Mount Tabor with ten thousand men following him.
>
> **4:15** The Lord routed Sisera, all his chariotry, and all his army with the edge of the sword. Sisera jumped out of his chariot and ran away on foot.
>
> **4:16** Now Barak chased the chariots and the army all the way to Harosheth Haggoyim. Sisera's whole army died by the edge of the sword; not even one survived.

Do you see any indication that Deborah actually engaged in battle?

_____

_____

2. Now read Hebrews 11:32–33 and consider:

Hebrews 11:32 And what more shall I say? For time will fail me if I tell of Gideon, Barak, Samson, Jephthah, of David and Samuel and the prophets.

11:33 Through faith they conquered kingdoms, administered justice, gained what was promised, shut the mouths of lions.

Gideon fought, Barak fought, Samson fought, and Jephthah fought. David killed Goliath, and Samuel killed Agag, king of the Amalekites. But did Deborah conquer with the sword? No. Some have suggested that the exclusion of Deborah from this "Faith Hall of Fame" list in Hebrews 11 means she was not the "real" judge, that Barak was the judge. Or they say that a woman leading was wrong and so she was excluded from the list. Yet the writer of Judges refers only to Deborah as the judge to whom the word of the Lord came (Judg. 4:4, 6). While Deborah went with the army, she did not engage in battle. Perhaps the New Testament writer meant to list only those who literally conquered kingdoms. While it's not entirely clear why Deborah is not listed in Hebrews 11, we must avoid reading too much into her absence. Stellar examples of faith such as Joseph, Daniel, and Mary, to name a few, are not mentioned either.

3. Deborah's story has often been at the center of the battle over what God does and doesn't want women to do in service to Him. But sadly, the focus can become so limited to gender issues that we miss the overall message of the story, which is not about gender at all. It's about God. Re-read Judges 4—5. Then summarize what you think God is trying to say to His people through the two versions, narrative and poetry, of the story:

_____

_____

_____

_____

_____

What a woman, that Deborah! First she was a prophet and probably a wife. In Hebrew the same word is used for "woman" and "wife," so we don't know for certain if Deborah was a "woman of Lappidoth" (a place) or "wife of Lappidoth" (a person) (Judg. 4:4). But most likely Deborah was married. The whole reason "woman" and "wife" weren't separate words in Deborah's day was because a female could be one of three things: a virgin, a married woman, or widowed. Deciding to live single was not on a woman's list of options unless her husband had died and left her enough sons to keep feeding her.

We know that Deborah was "a mother in Israel" (5:7). Yet we don't know for certain if that means she was a biological mother. More likely "a mother in Israel" is a title indicating that the nation looked to Deborah for leadership as the nation's mother similarly to how the childless George Washington could be called "the father or our nation" for Americans."

Deborah was also a judge. And she was a singer and songwriter.

She had an impressive résumé.

So when Deborah warned Barak that his conditional obedience would mean that the glory for defeating Sisera would go to a woman (4:9), we might assume she was referring to herself getting the glory for going with him. But Deborah was not speaking of herself at all. She was actually prophesying Sisera's death at the hands of tent-peg-wielding Jael.

So if the honor going to a woman was "God's punishment" for Barak's lack of faith, what does that say in general about a woman being more honored than a man? Precisely nothing. Elizabeth had more faith than Zechariah. Mary is better remembered than Joseph. Several times Paul mentioned Priscilla before her husband, Aquilla.

Just because it was dishonoring to be outdone by women in Deborah's day, that doesn't mean God sees women as "less."

Allow me a contemporary illustration.

A little more than thirty years ago a young athletic star named Billie Jean King was challenged to a tennis match in what was billed as the "Battle of the Sexes" exhibition. Another American tennis star, Bobby Riggs, 55, had been considered the best player in the world years earlier when he won Wimbledon and three U.S. Open championships. But years later he thought he still "had it" and could beat a 29-year-old—because she was a woman. Riggs even practiced in a Tshirt that said "If I am to be a chauvinist pig, I want to be the number-one pig."

Before a live audience of thirty thousand and a viewer audience of about fifty million, King soundly trounced Riggs in consecutive sets 6-4, 6-3, and 6-3.

Riggs was humiliated, as the match actually advanced the argument that a young woman could beat an older man—something few people today would even question. Clearly the honor went to a woman.

Was Riggs humiliated because a woman winning goes against nature? Or was his humiliation due in part to his erroneous views of women?

God got His message through to Barak in a way that Barak would understand: You lack faith—you lose honor. Rather than seeing this as a battle-of-the-sexes message, we need to see the much more significant spiritual message.

When you know what God wants you to do but tell Him, "I'll obey if . . ." you've put conditions on your obedience. And when you put conditions on your obedience, God doesn't lose—*you* do.

Prayer: *Heavenly Father, thank You for making me a woman. And thank You for Jesus, who revealed to a Samaritan woman that He was the Messiah, even when the disciples couldn't understand why He would speak to a female. Thank You for using Deborah and Jael to help deliver Your people from oppression. Use me in the battle against evil. Remove the obstacles in my life that keep me from absolute obedience to You. Help me never to put conditions on my obedience but always to be ready to respond immediately to the promptings of the Spirit. In the name of Your Son I pray. Amen.*

For Memorization: *"Hear, O kings! Pay attention, O rulers! I will sing to the Lord! I will sing to the Lord God of Israel!"* (Judg. 5:3)

WEEK 3 OF 6

Gideon: Judges 6–9

SUNDAY: HIS FLEECE WAS WET AS SNOW

Scripture: "Gideon said to God, 'Please do not get mad at me, when I ask for just one more sign. Please allow me one more test with the fleece. This time make just the fleece dry, while the ground around it is covered with dew.'" (Judg. 6:39)

"Dear Lord, if you want me to marry Carrie, please have her mention Proverbs 31 when I see her tonight."

This was the prayer of one of my college friends. He called it his "fleece." That is, in the same way Gideon wanted God to make a fleece wet to confirm His command with a sign, my friend came up with what he considered a modern-day way to determine God's will about whom to marry.

This friend, having prayed his fleece prayer, then sat with Carrie, my roommate, and peppered her with questions about her favorite Bible verses. When that evoked the wrong verses, he asked her views on women's ministry. Finally, he wanted to know what she thought about God's ideal in women. Suddenly he got the response he sought. She mentioned Proverbs 31.

"That's it!" he thought. "She must be the one for me!"

But they broke up a few months later, and Carrie went on to marry someone else.

At the time, I was too troubled by this guy's failure to follow God's apparently revealed will to see that he had badly mishandled and misapplied scripture. Laying out a fleece-equivalent is a way to put God to the test (something we're not supposed to do); it's not a way to find out what He wants.

Think about it. God had already told Gideon what He wanted him to do—fight the Midianites. And Gideon was too chicken to do it, so he demanded a sign of confirmation.

So the first principle we should take from the text if we're going to do a fleece-equivalent is that it must be to confirm something God has already commanded us to do. It might go something like this: "Lord, if You want me to be faithful to my husband, make the wool dry tonight" or "If You really want me to pray without ceasing, make the dry wool wet." Gideon's fleece was about something he already knew he was supposed to do. So principle number one: Use the fleece method only when you already know God's will.

Second, the sign from God must be supernatural. It can't be something like "If I'm supposed to give money to Your work regularly, let the traffic light turn green." It would need to be more like "If I'm supposed to give money to Your work regularly, let the traffic light turn purple." Gideon's confirmation required a miracle, not an everyday event.

When Gideon laid out his fleece, he asked that the Lord not become angry. That's because Gideon wasn't supposed to do it, and he knew it. The test demonstrated his lack of faith. And Jesus was quite clear that we're not to put God to the test (Matt. 4:7).

In his book *How to Read the Bible as Literature*, Leland Ryken writes,

> Some of the most foolish misreadings of biblical stories I have encountered has come from a misguided assumption that we are intended to approve of the behavior of biblical heroes in virtually every episode in which they figure. One of the distinctive features of the Bible is how deeply flawed its heroes and heroines are. The Bible portrays most of its protagonists as Cromwell wished to be painted—warts and all[3]

[3] Leland Ryken, *How to Read the Bible as Literature* (Grand Rapids: Zondervan, 1984), 77.

I am reminded of a student who prayed and prayed about where he should go to college. The desire to know the will of God, which was seemingly a mystery, drove him. He visited schools, pored over catalogs, and longed for God to write the "where" in the sky. Finally he selected a university.

During his first semester at school, he got involved with a bad crowd. Before long he was going on drinking binges and blowing off class. To no one's surprise, he flunked out. And do you know what he said? "I must have chosen the wrong school—I must have misread where I was supposed to go."

We do the same when we act immature in our marriages and then wonder if we married the wrong guy.

So often we focus on what job to take or whom to marry or where to live, when the Bible says, "This is the will of God—your sanctification" (1 Thess. 4:3). Where I am ranks as less important to God than who I am wherever I go. My choice of a spouse, while important, is still less important than the character I have as a wife. The company for which I work is less important than what kind of employee I am, regardless of where I work.

Are you struggling to know God's will? Maybe He's revealed it already. Be holy. Be sanctified. Love others. Speak only words that will edify. Rejoice always. Pray without ceasing. As far as it depends on you, be at peace with everyone. The other stuff, like who, what, and where—they're just the details.

MONDAY: OVERVIEW

1. After praying for supernatural guidance, read Judges 6—9.

Judges 6

6:1 The Israelites did evil in the Lord's sight, so the Lord turned them over to Midian for seven years. **6:2** The Midianite overwhelmed Israel. Because of Midian the Israelites made shelters for themselves in the hills, as well as caves and strongholds. **6:3** Whenever the Israelites planted their crops, the Midianites, Amalekites, and people from the east would attack them. **6:4** They invaded the land and devoured its crops all the way to Gaza. They left nothing for the Israelites to eat, and they took away the sheep, oxen, and donkeys. **6:5** When they invaded with their cattle and tents, they were as thick as locusts. Neither they nor their camels could be counted. They came to devour the land. **6:6** Israel was so severely weakened by Midian that the Israelites cried out to the Lord for help.

6:7 When the Israelites cried out to the Lord for help because of Midian, **6:8** he sent a prophet to the Israelites. He said to them, "This is what the Lord God of Israel says: 'I brought you up from Egypt and took you out of that place of slavery. **6:9** I rescued you from Egypt's power and from the power of all who oppressed you. I drove them out before you and gave their land to you. **6:10** I said to you, "I am the Lord your God! Do not worship the gods of the Amorites, in whose land you are now living!" But you have disobeyed me.'"

6:11 The Lord's angelic messenger came and sat down under the oak tree in Ophrah owned by Joash the Abiezrite. He arrived while Joash's son Gideon was threshing wheat in a winepress so he could hide it from the Midianites. **6:12** The Lord's messenger appeared and said to him, "The Lord is with you, courageous warrior!" **6:13** Gideon said to him, "Pardon me, but if the Lord is with us, why has such disaster overtaken us? Where are all his miraculous deeds our ancestors told us about? They said, 'Did the Lord not bring us up from Egypt?' But now the Lord has abandoned us and handed us over to Midian." **6:14** Then the Lord himself turned to him and said, "You have the strength. Deliver Israel from the power of the Midianites! Have I not sent you?" **6:15** Gideon said to him, "But Lord, how can I deliver Israel? Just look! My clan is the weakest in Manasseh, and I am the youngest in my family." **6:16** The Lord said to him, "Ah, but I will be with you! You will strike down the whole Midianite army." **6:17** Gideon said to him, "If you really are pleased with me, then give me a sign as proof that it is really you speaking with me. **6:18** Do not leave this place until I come back with a gift and present it to you." The Lord said, "I will stay here until you come back."

6:19 Gideon went and prepared a young goat, along with unleavened bread made from an ephah of flour. He put the meat in a basket and the broth in a pot. He brought the food to him under the oak tree and presented it to him. **6:20** God's messenger said to him, "Put the meat and unleavened bread on this rock, and pour out the broth." Gideon did as instructed. **6:21** The Lord's messenger touched the meat and the unleavened bread with the tip of his staff. Fire flared up from the rock and consumed the meat and unleavened bread. The Lord's messenger then disappeared.

6:22 When Gideon realized that it was the Lord's messenger, he said, "Oh no! Master, Lord! I have seen the Lord's messenger face to face!" **6:23** The Lord said to him, "You are safe! Do not be afraid! You are not going to die!" **6:24** Gideon built an altar for the Lord there, and named it "The Lord is on friendly terms with me." To this day it is still there in Ophrah of the Abiezrites.

6:25 That night the Lord said to him, "Take the bull from your father's herd, as well as a second bull, one that is seven years old. Pull down your father's Baal altar and cut down the nearby Asherah pole. **6:26** Then build an altar for the Lord your God on the top of this stronghold according to the proper pattern. Take the second bull and offer it as a burnt sacrifice on the wood from the Asherah pole that you cut down." **6:27** So Gideon took ten of his servants and did just as the Lord had told him. He was too afraid of his father's family and the men of the city to do it in broad daylight, so he waited until nighttime.

6:28 When the men of the city got up the next morning, they saw the Baal altar pulled down, the nearby Asherah pole cut down, and the second bull sacrificed on the newly built altar. **6:29** They said to one another, "Who did this?" They investigated the matter thoroughly and concluded that Gideon son of Joash had done it. **6:30** The men of the city said to Joash, "Bring out your son, so we can execute him! He pulled down the Baal altar and cut down the nearby Asherah pole." **6:31** But Joash said to all those who confronted him, "Must you fight Baal's battles? Must you rescue him? Whoever takes up his cause will die by morning! If he really is a god, let him fight his own battles! After all, it was his altar that was pulled down." **6:32** That very day Gideon's father named him Jerub-Baal, because he had said, "Let Baal fight with him, for it was his altar that was pulled down."

6:33 All the Midianites, Amalekites, and the people from the east assembled. They crossed the Jordan River and camped in the Jezreel Valley. **6:34** The Lord's spirit took control of Gideon. He blew a trumpet, summoning the Abiezrites to follow him. **6:35** He sent messengers throughout Manasseh and summoned them to follow him as well. He also sent messengers throughout Asher, Zebulun, and Naphtali, and they came up to meet him.

6:36 Gideon said to God, "If you really intend to use me to deliver Israel, as you promised, then give me a sign as proof. **6:37** Look, I am putting a wool fleece on the threshing floor. If there is dew on just the fleece, and the ground around it is dry, then I will be sure that you will use me to deliver Israel, as you promised." **6:38** The Lord did as he asked. When he got up the next morning, he squeezed the fleece, and enough dew dripped from it to fill a bowl. **6:39** Gideon said to God, "Please do not get mad at me, when I ask for just one more sign. Please allow me one more test with the fleece. This time make just the fleece dry, while the ground around it is covered with dew. **6:40** That night God did as he asked. Just the fleece was dry and the ground around it was covered with dew.

Judges 7

7:1 Jerub-Baal (that is, Gideon) and his men got up the next morning and camped near the spring of Harod. The Midianites were camped north of them near the hill of Moreh in the valley. **7:2** The Lord said to Gideon, "You have too many men for me to hand Midian over to you. Israel might brag, 'Our own strength has delivered us.' **7:3** Now, announce to the men, 'Whoever is shaking with fear may turn around and leave Mount Gilead.'" Twenty-two thousand men went home; ten thousand remained. **7:4** The Lord spoke to Gideon again, "There are still too many men. Bring them down to the water and I will thin the ranks some more. When I say, 'This one should go with you,' pick him to go; when I say, 'This one should not go with you,' do not take him." **7:5** So he brought the men down to the water. Then the Lord said to Gideon, "Separate those who lap the water as a dog laps from those kneel to drink." **7:6** Three hundred men lapped; the rest of the men kneeled to drink water. **7:7** The Lord said to Gideon, "With the three hundred men who lapped I will deliver the whole army and I will hand Midian over to you. The rest of the men should go home." **7:8** The men who were chosen took supplies and their trumpets. Gideon sent all the men of Israel back to their homes; he kept only three hundred men. Now the Midianites were camped down below in the valley.

7:9 That night the Lord said to Gideon, "Get up! Attack the camp, for I am handing it over to you. **7:10** But if you are afraid to attack, go down to the camp with Purah your servant **7:11** and listen to what they are saying. Then you will be brave and attack the camp." So he went down with Purah his servant to where the sentries were guarding the camp. **7:12** Now the Midianites, Amalekites, and people from the east covered the valley like a swarm of locusts. Their camels could not be counted; they were as innumerable as the sand on the seashore. **7:13** When Gideon arrived, he heard a man telling another man about a dream he had. The man said, "Look! I had a dream. I saw a stale cake of barley bread rolling into the Midianite camp. It hit a tent so hard it knocked it over and turned it upside down. The tent just collapsed." **7:14** The other man said, "Without a doubt this symbolizes the sword of Gideon son of Joash, the Israelite. God is handing Midian and all the army over to him."

7:15 When Gideon heard the report of the dream and its interpretation, he praised God. Then he went back to the Israelite camp and said, "Get up, for the Lord is handing the Midianite army over to you!" **7:16** He divided the three hundred men into three units. He gave them all trumpets and empty jars with torches inside them. **7:17** He said to them, "Watch me and do as I do. Watch closely! I am going to the edge of the camp. Do as I do! **7:18** When I and all who are with me blow our trumpets, you also blow your trumpets all around the camp. Then say, 'For the Lord and for Gideon!'"

7:19 Gideon took a hundred men to the edge of the camp at the beginning of the middle watch, just after they had changed the guards. They blew their trumpets and broke the jars they were carrying. **7:20** All three units blew their trumpets and broke their jars. They held the torches in their left hand and the trumpets in their right. Then they yelled, "A sword for the Lord and for Gideon!" **7:21** They stood in order all around the camp. The whole army ran away; they shouted as they scrambled away. **7:22** When the three hundred men blew their trumpets, the Lord caused the Midianites to attack one another with their swords throughout the camp. The army fled to Beth Shittah on the way to Zererah. They went to the border of Abel Meholah near Tabbath. **7:23** Israelites from Naphtali, Asher, and Manasseh answered the call and chased the Midianites.

7:24 Now Gideon sent messengers throughout the Ephraimite hill country who announced, "Go down and head off the Midianites. Take control of the fords of the streams all the way to Beth Barah and the Jordan River." When all the Ephraimites had assembled, they took control of the fords all the way to Beth Barah and the Jordan River. **7:25** They captured the two Midianite generals, Oreb and Zeeb. They executed Oreb on the rock of Oreb and Zeeb in the winepress of Zeeb. They chased the Midianites and brought the heads of Oreb and Zeeb to Gideon, who was now on the other side of the Jordan River.

Judges 8

8:1 The Ephraimites said to him, "Why have you done such a thing to us?" You did not summon us when you went to fight the Midianites!" They argued vehemently with him. **8:2** He said to them, "Now what have I accomplished compared to you? Even Ephraim's leftover grapes are better quality than Abiezer's harvest! **8:3** It was to you that God handed over the Midianite generals, Oreb and Zeeb! What did I accomplish to rival that?" When he said this, they calmed down.

8:4 Now Gideon and his three hundred men had crossed over the Jordan River and, though exhausted, were still chasing the Midianites. **8:5** He said to the men of Succoth, "Give some loaves of bread to the men who are following me, because they are exhausted. I am chasing Zebah and Zalmunna, the kings of Midian." **8:6** The officials of Succoth said, "You have not yet overpowered Zebah and Zalmunna. So why should we give bread to your army?" **8:7** Gideon said, "Since you will not help, after the Lord hands Zebah and Zalmunna over to me, I will thresh your skin with desert thorns and briers." **8:8** He went up from there to Penuel and made the same request. The men of Penuel responded the same way the men of Succoth had. **8:9** He also threatened the men of Penuel, warning, "When I return victoriously, I will tear down this tower."

8:10 Now Zebah and Zalmunna were in Karkor with their armies. There were about fifteen thousand survivors from the army of the eastern peoples; a hundred and twenty thousand sword-wielding soldiers had been killed. **8:11** Gideon went up the road of the nomads east of Nobah and Jogbehah and ambushed the surprised army. **8:12** When Zebah and Zalmunna ran away, Gideon chased them and captured the two Midianite kings, Zebah and Zalmunna. He had surprised their entire army.

8:13 Gideon son of Joash returned from the battle by the pass of Heres. **8:14** He captured a young man from Succoth and interrogated him. The young man wrote down for him the names of Succoth's officials and city leaders—seventy-seven men in all. **8:15** He approached the men of Succoth and said, "Look what I have! Zebah and Zalmunna! You insulted me, saying, 'You have not yet overpowered Zebah and Zalmunna. So why should we give bread to your exhausted men?'" **8:16** He grabbed the leaders of the city, along with some desert thorns and briers; he then "threshed" the men of Succoth with them. **8:17** He also tore down the tower of Penuel and executed the city's men.

8:18 He said to Zebah and Zalmunna, "Describe for me the men you killed at Tabor." They said, "They were like you. Each one looked like a king's son." **8:19** He said, "They were my brothers, the sons of my mother. I swear, as surely as the Lord is alive, if you had let them live, I would not kill you." **8:20** He ordered Jether his firstborn son, "Come on! Kill them!" But Jether was too afraid to draw his sword, because he was still young. **8:21** Zebah and Zalmunna said to Gideon, "Come on, you strike us, for a man is judged by his strength." So Gideon killed Zebah and Zalmunna, and he took the crescent-shaped ornaments which were on the necks of their camels.

8:22 The men of Israel said to Gideon, "Rule over us—you, your son, and your grandson. For you have delivered us from Midian's power." **8:23** Gideon said to them, "I will not rule over you, nor will my son rule over you. The Lord will rule over you." **8:24** Gideon continued, "I would like to make one request. Each of you give me an earring from the plunder you have taken." (The Midianites had gold earrings because they were Ishmaelites.) **8:25** They said, "We are happy to give you earrings." So they spread out a garment, and each one threw an earring from his plunder onto it. **8:26** The total weight of the gold earrings he requested came to seventeen hundred gold shekels. This was in addition to the crescent-shaped ornaments, jewelry, purple clothing worn by the Midianite kings, and the necklaces on the camels. **8:27** Gideon used all this to make an ephod, which he put in his hometown of Ophrah. All the Israelites prostituted themselves to it there. It became a snare to Gideon and his family.

8:28 The Israelites humiliated Midian; the Midianites' fighting spirit was broken. The land had rest for forty years during Gideon's time. **8:29** Then Jerub-Baal son of Joash went home and settled down. **8:30** Gideon fathered seventy sons through his many wives. **8:31** His concubine, who lived in Shechem, also gave him a son, whom he named Abimelech. **8:32** Gideon son of Joash died at a very old age and was buried in the tomb of his father Joash located in Ophrah of the Abiezrites.

8:33 After Gideon died, the Israelites again prostituted themselves to the Baals. They made Baal-Berith their god. **8:34** The Israelites did not remain true to the Lord their God, who had delivered them from all the enemies who lived around them. **8:35** They did not treat the family of Jerub-Baal (that is, Gideon) fairly in return for all the good he had done for Israel.

Judges 9

9:1 Now Abimelech son of Jerub-Baal went to Shechem to see his mother's relatives. He said to them and to his mother's entire extended family, **9:2** "Tell all the leaders of Shechem this: 'Why would you want to have seventy men, all Jerub-Baal's sons, ruling over you, when you can have just one ruler? Recall that I am your own flesh and blood.' " **9:3** His mother's relatives spoke on his behalf to all the leaders of Shechem and reported his proposal. The leaders were drawn to Abimelech; they said, "He is our close relative." **9:4** They paid him seventy silver shekels out of the temple of Baal-Berith. Abimelech then used the silver to hire some lawless, dangerous men as his followers. **9:5** He went to his father's home in Ophrah and murdered his half-brothers, the seventy legitimate sons of Jerub-Baal, on one stone. Only Jotham, Jerub-Baal's youngest son, escaped, because he hid. **9:6** All the leaders of Shechem and Beth Millo assembled and then went and made Abimelech king by the oak near the pillar in Shechem.

9:7 When Jotham heard the news, he went and stood on the top of Mount Gerizim. He spoke loudly to the people below, "Listen to me, leaders of Shechem, so that God may listen to you!

9:8 "The trees were determined to go out and choose a king for themselves. They said to the olive tree, 'Be our king!' **9:9** But the olive tree said to them, 'I am not going to stop producing my oil, which is used to honor gods and men, just to sway above the other trees!'

9:10 "So the trees said to the fig tree, 'You come and be our king!' **9:11** But the fig tree said to them, 'I am not going to stop producing my sweet figs, my excellent fruit, just to sway above the other trees!'

9:12 "So the trees said to the grapevine, 'You come and be our king!' **9:13** But the grapevine said to them, 'I am not going to stop producing my wine, which makes gods and men so happy, just to sway above the other trees!'

9:14 "So all the trees said to the thornbush, 'You come and be our king!' **9:15** The thornbush said to the trees, 'If you really want to choose me as your king, then come along, find safety under my branches! Otherwise may fire blaze from the thornbush and consume the cedars of Lebanon!'

9:16 "Now, if you have shown loyalty and integrity when you made Abimelech king, if you have done right to Jerub-Baal and his family, if you have properly repaid him—**9:17** my father fought for you; he risked his life and delivered you from Midian's power. **9:18** But you have attacked my father's family today. You murdered his seventy legitimate sons on one stone and made Abimelech, the son of his female slave, king over the leaders of Shechem, just because he is your close relative. **9:19** So if you have shown loyalty and integrity to Jerub-Baal and his family today, then may Abimelech bring you happiness and may you bring him happiness! **9:20** But if not, may fire blaze from Abimelech and consume the leaders of Shechem and Beth Millo! May fire also blaze from the leaders of Shechem and Beth Millo and consume Abimelech!" **9:21** Then Jotham ran away to Beer and lived there to escape from Abimelech his half-brother.

9:22 Abimelech commanded Israel for three years. **9:23** God sent a spirit to stir up hostility between Abimelech and the leaders of Shechem. He made the leaders of Shechem disloyal to Abimelech. **9:24** He did this so the violent deaths of Jerub-Baal's seventy sons might be avenged and Abimelech, their half-brother who murdered them, might have to pay for their spilled blood, along with the leaders of Shechem who helped him murder them. **9:25** The leaders of Shechem rebelled against Abimelech by putting bandits in the hills, who robbed everyone who traveled by on the road. But Abimelech found out about it.

9:26 Gaal son of Ebed came through Shechem with his brothers. The leaders of Shechem transferred their loyalty to him. **9:27** They went out to the field, harvested their grapes, squeezed out the juice, and celebrated. They came to the temple of their god and ate, drank, and cursed Abimelech. **9:28** Gaal son of Ebed said, "Who is Abimelech and who is Shechem, that we should serve him? Is he not the son of Jerub-Baal, and is not Zebul the deputy he appointed? Serve the sons of Hamor, the father of Shechem! But why should we serve Abimelech? **9:29** If only these men were under my command, I would get rid of Abimelech!" He challenged Abimelech, "Muster your army and come out for battle!"

9:30 When Zebul, the city commissioner, heard the words of Gaal son of Ebed, he was furious. **9:31** He sent messengers to Abimelech, who was in Arumah, reporting, "Beware! Gaal son of Ebed and his brothers are coming to Shechem and inciting the city to rebel against you. **9:32** Now, come up at night with your men and set an ambush in the field outside the city. **9:33** In the morning at sunrise quickly attack the city. When he and his men come out to fight you, do what you can to him."

9:34 So Abimelech and all his men came up at night and set an ambush outside Shechem—they divided into four units. **9:35** When Gaal son of Ebed came out and stood at the entrance to the city's gate, Abimelech and his men got up from their hiding places. **9:36** Gaal saw the men and said to Zebul, "Look, men are coming down from the tops of the hills." But Zebul said to him, "You are seeing the shadows on the hills—it just looks like men." **9:37** Gaal again said, "Look, men are coming down from the very center of the land. A unit is coming by way of the Oak Tree of the Diviners. **9:38** Zebul said to him, "Where now are your bragging words, 'Who is Abimelech that we should serve him?' Are these not the men you insulted? Go out now and fight them!" **9:39** So Gaal led the leaders of Shechem out and fought Abimelech. **9:40** Abimelech chased him, and Gaal ran from him. Many Shechemites fell wounded at the opening of the gate. **9:41** Abimelech went back to Arumah; Zebul drove Gaal and his brothers out of Shechem.

9:42 The next day the Shechemites came out to the field. When Abimelech heard about it, **9:43** he took his men and divided them into three units and set an ambush in the field. When he saw the people coming out of the city, he attacked and struck them down. **9:44** Abimelech and his units attacked and blocked the entrance to the city's gate. Two units then attacked all the people in the field and struck them down. **9:45** Abimelech fought against the city all that day. He captured the city and killed all the people in it. Then he leveled the city and spread salt over it.

9:46 When all the leaders of the Tower of Shechem heard the news, they went to the stronghold of the temple of El-Berith. **9:47** Abimelech heard that all the leaders of the Tower of Shechem were in one place. **9:48** He and all his men went up on Mount Zalmon. He took an ax in his hand and cut off a tree branch. He put it on his shoulder and said to his men, "Quickly, do what you have just seen me do!" **9:49** So each of his men also cut off a branch and followed Abimelech. They put the branches against the stronghold and set fire to it. All the people of the Tower of Shechem died—about a thousand men and women.

9:50 Abimelech moved on to Thebez; he besieged and captured it. **9:51** There was a fortified tower in the center of the city, so all the men and women, as well as the city's leaders, ran into it and locked the entrance. Then they went up to the roof of the tower. **9:52** Abimelech came and attacked the tower. When he approached the entrance of the tower to set it on fire, **9:53** a woman threw an upper millstone down on his head and shattered his skull. **9:54** He quickly called to the young man who carried his weapons, "Draw your sword and kill me, so they will not say, 'A woman killed him.'" So the young man stabbed him and he died. **9:55** When the Israelites saw that Abimelech was dead, they went home.

9:56 God repaid Abimelech for the evil he did to his father by murdering his seventy half-brothers. **9:57** God also repaid the men of Shechem for their evil deeds. The curse spoken by Jotham son of Jerub-Baal fell on them.

2. Note observations of particular interest, or write questions you have:

_____

_____

_____

_____

_____

1. Re-read Judges 6:11–40.

Judges 6:11 The Lord's angelic messenger came and sat down under the oak tree in Ophrah owned by Joash the Abiezrite. He arrived while Joash's son Gideon was threshing wheat in a winepress so he could hide it from the Midianites. **6:12** The Lord's messenger appeared and said to him, "The Lord is with you, courageous warrior!" **6:13** Gideon said to him, "Pardon me, but if the Lord is with us, why has such disaster overtaken us? Where are all his miraculous deeds our ancestors told us about? They said, 'Did the Lord not bring us up from Egypt?' But now the Lord has abandoned us and handed us over to Midian." **6:14** Then the Lord himself turned to him and said, "You have the strength. Deliver Israel from the power of the Midianites! Have I not sent you?" **6:15** Gideon said to him, "But Lord, how can I deliver Israel? Just look! My clan is the weakest in Manasseh, and I am the youngest in my family." **6:16** The Lord said to him, "Ah, but I will be with you! You will strike down the whole Midianite army." **6:17** Gideon said to him, "If you really are pleased with me, then give me a sign as proof that it is really you speaking with me. **6:18** Do not leave this place until I come back with a gift and present it to you." The Lord said, "I will stay here until you come back."

6:19 Gideon went and prepared a young goat, along with unleavened bread made from an ephah of flour. He put the meat in a basket and the broth in a pot. He brought the food to him under the oak tree and presented it to him. **6:20** God's messenger said to him, "Put the meat and unleavened bread on this rock, and pour out the broth." Gideon did as instructed. **6:21** The Lord's messenger touched the meat and the unleavened bread with the tip of his staff. Fire flared up from the rock and consumed the meat and unleavened bread. The Lord's messenger then disappeared.

6:22 When Gideon realized that it was the Lord's messenger, he said, "Oh no! Master, Lord! I have seen the Lord's messenger face to face!" **6:23** The Lord said to him, "You are safe! Do not be afraid!

You are not going to die!" **6:24** Gideon built an altar for the Lord there, and named it "The Lord is on friendly terms with me." To this day it is still there in Ophrah of the Abiezrites.

6:25 That night the Lord said to him, "Take the bull from your father's herd, as well as a second bull, one that is seven years old. Pull down your father's Baal altar and cut down the nearby Asherah pole. **6:26** Then build an altar for the Lord your God on the top of this stronghold according to the proper pattern. Take the second bull and offer it as a burnt sacrifice on the wood from the Asherah pole that you cut down." **6:27** So Gideon took ten of his servants and did just as the Lord had told him. He was too afraid of his father's family and the men of the city to do it in broad daylight, so he waited until nighttime.

6:28 When the men of the city got up the next morning, they saw the Baal altar pulled down, the nearby Asherah pole cut down, and the second bull sacrificed on the newly built altar. **6:29** They said to one another, "Who did this?" They investigated the matter thoroughly and concluded that Gideon son of Joash had done it. **6:30** The men of the city said to Joash, "Bring out your son, so we can execute him! He pulled down the Baal altar and cut down the nearby Asherah pole." **6:31** But Joash said to all those who con-fronted him, "Must you fight Baal's battles? Must you rescue him? Whoever takes up his cause will die by morning! If he really is a god, let him fight his own battles! After all, it was his altar that was pulled down." **6:32** That very day Gideon's father named him Jerub-Baal, because he had said, "Let Baal fight with him, for it was his altar that was pulled down."

6:33 All the Midianites, Amalekites, and the people from the east assembled. They crossed the Jordan River and camped in the Jezreel Valley. **6:34** The Lord's spirit took control of Gideon. He blew a trumpet, summoning the Abiezrites to follow him. **6:35** He sent messengers throughout Manasseh and summoned them to follow him as well. He also sent messengers throughout Asher, Zebulun, and Naphtali, and they came up to meet him.

6:36 Gideon said to God, "If you really intend to use me to deliver Israel, as you promised, then give me a sign as proof. **6:37** Look, I am putting a wool fleece on the threshing floor. If there is dew on just the fleece, and the ground around it is dry, then I will be sure that you will use me to deliver Israel, as you promised." **6:38** The Lord did as he asked. When he got up the next morning, he squeezed the fleece, and enough dew dripped from it to fill a bowl. **6:39** Gideon said to God, "Please do not get mad at me, when I ask for just one more sign. Please allow me one more test with the fleece. This time make just the fleece dry, while the ground around it is covered with dew. **6:40** That night God did as he asked. Just the fleece was dry and the ground around it was covered with dew.

2. God clearly revealed His will to Gideon. What was it (6:14)?

_____

_____

3. Now re-read 6:36–40.

> **Judges 6:36** Gideon said to God, "If you really intend to use me to deliver Israel, as you promised, then give me a sign as proof. **6:37** Look, I am putting a wool fleece on the threshing floor. If there is dew on just the fleece, and the ground around it is dry, then I will be sure that you will use me to deliver Israel, as you promised." **6:38** The Lord did as he asked. When he got up the next morning, he squeezed the fleece, and enough dew dripped from it to fill a bowl. **6:39** Gideon said to God, "Please do not get mad at me, when I ask for just one more sign. Please allow me one more test with the fleece. This time make just the fleece dry, while the ground around it is covered with dew. **6:40** That night God did as he asked. Just the fleece was dry and the ground around it was covered with dew.

A. What was Gideon's attitude about asking a second time?

_____

_____

_____

B. What was God's response?

_____

_____

_____

C. Does the fact that God answered the way He did suggest that Gideon was right to doubt?

_____

_____

_____

4. Note the times God's people said "if" (Judges 4:8; 6:17, 36–37, emphasis added in all three quotations).

> **4:8** Barak said to her, "**If** you go with me, I will go. But if you do not go with me, I will not go."
>
> **6:17** Gideon said to him, "**If** if you really are pleased with me, then give me a sign as proof that it is really you speaking with me. **6:18** Do not leave this place until I come back with a gift and present it to you."
>
> **6:36** Gideon said to God, "**If** you really intend to use me to deliver Israel as you have promised then give me a sign as proof. **6:37** Look, I am putting a wool fleece on the threshing floor. **If** there is dew on just the fleece, and the ground around it is dry, then I will be sure that you will use me to deliver Israel, as you promised."

Are there areas of your life in which you find yourself negotiating with God rather than obeying? If so, what are they?

_____

_____

_____

_____

5. What has God already commanded that you need to obey?

_____

_____

6. Think about how you make decisions. Do you seek counsel, pray, read the Bible, maybe fast, and try to act wisely, or do you ask for God to give quick signs? What are some decisions you currently face? Ask for wisdom and guidance. What guidance, if any, has He already provided?

WEDNESDAY: THE GOD OF THE SMALL

If how to know God's will is not the point of this passage, what *is* the point? Virtually everything points to Gideon's inadequacy in contrast with God's adequacy:

1. Re-read Judges 6.

2. What is ironic about how the angel greets Gideon as recorded in 6:12?

3. How does Gideon respond (vv. 13, 15)?

4. What does God promise (vv. 16–18.)?

_____

_____

_____

5. Why does Gideon choose to tear down his father's pagan altar at night instead of during the day (v. 27)?

_____

_____

_____

6. The story of David and Goliath has the same moral as Gideon's story—God's power is shown most mightily through an "underdog" who obeys Him. In what position are you weak? That is, what is the biggest obstacle, enemy, or challenge you face today?

_____

_____

_____

Spend some time praying that God will help you transfer your focus from your smallness to His greatness. If He can use Gideon, He can use you!

7. Is there someone who would benefit from your testimony? For example, if you face a health problem, who might benefit from hearing how God is sustaining you through it?

_____

_____

THURSDAY: STRENGTH MADE PERFECT IN WEAKNESS

1. Read Judges 7:1–8.

> **Judges 7:1** Jerub-Baal (that is, Gideon) and his men got up the next morning and camped near the spring of Harod. The Midianites were camped north of them near the hill of Moreh in the valley. **7:2** The Lord said to Gideon, "You have too many men for me to hand Midian over to you. Israel might brag, 'Our own strength has delivered us.' **7:3** Now, announce to the men, 'Whoever is shaking with fear may turn around and leave Mount Gilead.'" Twenty-two thousand men went home; ten thousand remained. **7:4** The Lord spoke to Gideon again, "There are still too many men. Bring them down to the water and I will thin the ranks some more. When I say, 'This one should go with you,' pick him to go; when I say, 'This one should not go with you,' do not take him." **7:5** So he brought the men down to the water. Then the Lord said to Gideon, "Separate those who lap the water as a dog laps from those kneel to drink." **7:6** Three hundred men lapped; the rest of the men kneeled to drink water. **7:7** The Lord said to Gideon, "With the three hundred men who lapped I will deliver the whole army and I will hand Midian over to you. The rest of the men should go home." **7:8** The men who were chosen took supplies and their trumpets. Gideon sent all the men of Israel back to their homes; he kept only three hundred men. Now the Midianites were camped down below in the valley.

2. Why didn't God want the army to be mighty? (v. 2.)

_____

_____

_____

3. Read Judges 7:9–25.

> **Judges 7:9** That night the Lord said to Gideon, "Get up! Attack the camp, for I am handing it over to you. **7:10** But if you are afraid

to attack, go down to the camp with Purah your servant **7:11** and listen to what they are saying. Then you will be brave and attack the camp." So he went down with Purah his servant to where the sentries were guarding the camp. **7:12** Now the Midianites, Amalekites, and people from the east covered the valley like a swarm of locusts. Their camels could not be counted; they were as innumerable as the sand on the seashore. **7:13** When Gideon arrived, he heard a man telling another man about a dream he had. The man said, "Look! I had a dream. I saw a stale cake of barley bread rolling into the Midianite camp. It hit a tent so hard it knocked it over and turned it upside down. The tent just collapsed." **7:14** The other man said, "Without a doubt this symbolizes the sword of Gideon son of Joash, the Israelite. God is handing Midian and all the army over to him."

7:15 When Gideon heard the report of the dream and its interpretation, he praised God. Then he went back to the Israelite camp and said, "Get up, for the Lord is handing the Midianite army over to you!" **7:16** He divided the three hundred men into three units. He gave them all trumpets and empty jars with torches inside them. **7:17** He said to them, "Watch me and do as I do. Watch closely! I am going to the edge of the camp. Do as I do! **7:18** When I and all who are with me blow our trumpets, you also blow your trumpets all around the camp. Then say, 'For the Lord and for Gideon!'"

7:19 Gideon took a hundred men to the edge of the camp at the beginning of the middle watch, just after they had changed the guards. They blew their trumpets and broke the jars they were carrying. **7:20** All three units blew their trumpets and broke their jars. They held the torches in their left hand and the trumpets in their right. Then they yelled, "A sword for the Lord and for Gideon!" **7:21** They stood in order all around the camp. The whole army ran away; they shouted as they scrambled away. **7:22** When the three hundred men blew their trumpets, the Lord caused the Midianites to attack one another with their swords throughout the camp. The army fled to Beth Shittah on the way to Zererah. They went to the border of Abel Meholah near Tabbath. **7:23** Israelites from Naphtali, Asher, and Manasseh answered the call and chased the Midianites.

7:24 Now Gideon sent messengers throughout the Ephraimite hill country who announced, "Go down and head off the Midianites. Take control of the fords of the streams all the way to Beth Barah and the Jordan River." When all the Ephraimites had assembled, they took control of the fords all the way to Beth Barah and the Jordan River. **7:25** They captured the two Midianite generals, Oreb and Zeeb. They executed Oreb on the rock of Oreb and Zeeb in the winepress of Zeeb. They chased the Midianites and brought the heads of Oreb and Zeeb to Gideon, who was now on the other side of the Jordan River.

What do we learn about God in this section?

_____

_____

_____

_____

_____

4. Read 2 Corinthians 12:7–10:

> **2 Corinthians 12:7** Therefore, so that I would not become arrogant, a thorn in the flesh was given to me, a messenger of Satan to trouble me—so that I would not become arrogant. **12:8** I asked the Lord three times about this, that it would depart from me. **12:9** But he said to me, "My grace is enough for you, for my power is made perfect in weakness." So then, I will boast most gladly about my weaknesses, so that the power of Christ may reside in me. **12:10** Therefore I am content with weaknesses, with insults, with troubles, with persecutions and difficulties for the sake of Christ, for whenever I am weak, then I am strong.

List some of your areas of weakness (financial difficulty, health problems, relational problems, sins with which you struggle).

_____

_____

_____

_____

5. Ask God to prove His strength in you through your weakness so He might get the glory.

6. Write down a time when God worked through you, even though you were reluctant or weak. What does this tell you about God?

_____

_____

_____

_____

7. Re-read Judges 8:22–35.

> **Judges 8:22** The men of Israel said to Gideon, "Rule over us—you, your son, and your grandson. For you have delivered us from Midian's power." **8:23** Gideon said to them, "I will not rule over you, nor will my son rule over you. The Lord will rule over you." **8:24** Gideon continued, "I would like to make one request. Each of you give me an earring from the plunder you have taken." (The Midianites had gold earrings because they were Ishmaelites.) **8:25** They said, "We are happy to give you earrings." So they spread out a garment, and each one threw an earring from his plunder onto it. **8:26** The total weight of the gold earrings he requested came to seventeen hundred gold shekels. This was in addition to the crescent-shaped ornaments, jewelry, purple clothing worn by the Midianite kings, and the necklaces on the camels. **8:27** Gideon used all this to make an ephod, which he put in his hometown of Ophrah. All the Israelites prostituted themselves to it there. It became a snare to Gideon and his family.
>
> **8:28** The Israelites humiliated Midian; the Midianites' fighting spirit was broken. The land had rest for forty years during Gideon's time. **8:29** Then Jerub-Baal son of Joash went home and settled down. **8:30** Gideon fathered seventy sons through his many wives. **8:31** His concubine, who lived in Shechem, also gave him a son, whom he named Abimelech. **8:32** Gideon son of Joash died at a very old age and was buried in the tomb of his father Joash located in Ophrah of the Abiezrites.
>
> **8:33** After Gideon died, the Israelites again prostituted themselves to the Baals. They made Baal-Berith their god. **8:34** The

Israelites did not remain true to the Lord their God, who had delivered them from all the enemies who lived around them. **8:35** They did not treat the family of Jerub-Baal (that is, Gideon) fairly in return for all the good he had done for Israel.

Down goes the spiral. God had told His people not to start a dynasty—that *He* was to be their ruler. Yet what did the people do (v. 22)?

_____

_____

_____

> Gideon did not want the responsibility of being a king, yet he did what kings do—he accumulated gold (8:24) and wives (8:30). This became a snare. He also named his son "Abimelech," which means "my father is king"! Although Gideon didn't start a dynasty, his son had other ideas after his father's death. By appealing to his family's power in Israel, Abimelech received silver from the idol temple treasury, and he killed all but one of Gideon's other seventy sons. In doing so he acted much like a Canaanite—actually worse, as he killed his own brothers instead of other nations' kings (see Judg. 1:5-7). He was made king and later killed by a woman (9:53).

8. The children of Israel wanted Gideon to rule them because he had led them in victory. But was it really Gideon who delivered Israel? Where is the victory song we saw in Judges 5 following success in battle? Against astounding odds, we see no praise, gratitude, or thanks offered to God. Gideon passed the test of adversity but was less successful in the test of prosperity. Do you find it easier to trust God when your life is going well or when you're facing trials? Why?

_____

_____

_____

_____

1. Re-read Judges 9.

Judges 9

9:1 Now Abimelech son of Jerub-Baal went to Shechem to see his mother's relatives. He said to them and to his mother's entire extended family, **9:2** "Tell all the leaders of Shechem this: 'Why would you want to have seventy men, all Jerub-Baal's sons, ruling over you, when you can have just one ruler? Recall that I am your own flesh and blood.'" **9:3** His mother's relatives spoke on his behalf to all the leaders of Shechem and reported his proposal. The leaders were drawn to Abimelech; they said, "He is our close relative." **9:4** They paid him seventy silver shekels out of the temple of Baal-Berith. Abimelech then used the silver to hire some lawless, dangerous men as his followers. **9:5** He went to his father's home in Ophrah and murdered his half-brothers, the seventy legitimate sons of Jerub-Baal, on one stone. Only Jotham, Jerub-Baal's youngest son, escaped, because he hid. **9:6** All the leaders of Shechem and Beth Millo assembled and then went and made Abimelech king by the oak near the pillar in Shechem.

9:7 When Jotham heard the news, he went and stood on the top of Mount Gerizim. He spoke loudly to the people below, "Listen to me, leaders of Shechem, so that God may listen to you!

9:8 "The trees were determined to go out and choose a king for themselves. They said to the olive tree, 'Be our king!' **9:9** But the olive tree said to them, 'I am not going to stop producing my oil, which is used to honor gods and men, just to sway above the other trees!'

9:10 "So the trees said to the fig tree, 'You come and be our king!' **9:11** But the fig tree said to them, 'I am not going to stop producing my sweet figs, my excellent fruit, just to sway above the other trees!'

9:12 "So the trees said to the grapevine, 'You come and be our king!' **9:13** But the grapevine said to them, 'I am not going to stop producing my wine, which makes gods and men so happy, just to sway above the other trees!'

9:14 "So all the trees said to the thornbush, 'You come and be our king!' **9:15** The thornbush said to the trees, 'If you really want to choose me as your king, then come along, find safety under my branches! Otherwise may fire blaze from the thornbush and consume the cedars of Lebanon!'

9:16 "Now, if you have shown loyalty and integrity when you made Abimelech king, if you have done right to Jerub-Baal and his family, if you have properly repaid him—**9:17** my father fought for you; he risked his life and delivered you from Midian's power. **9:18** But you have attacked my father's family today. You murdered his seventy legitimate sons on one stone and made Abimelech, the son of his female slave, king over the leaders of Shechem, just because he is your close relative. **9:19** So if you have shown loyalty and integrity to Jerub-Baal and his family today, then may Abimelech bring you happiness and may you bring him happiness! **9:20** But if not, may fire blaze from Abimelech and consume the leaders of Shechem and Beth Millo! May fire also blaze from the leaders of Shechem and Beth Millo and consume Abimelech!" **9:21** Then Jotham ran away to Beer and lived there to escape from Abimelech his half-brother.

9:22 Abimelech commanded Israel for three years. **9:23** God sent a spirit to stir up hostility between Abimelech and the leaders of Shechem. He made the leaders of Shechem disloyal to Abimelech. **9:24** He did this so the violent deaths of Jerub-Baal's seventy sons might be avenged and Abimelech, their half-brother who murdered them, might have to pay for their spilled blood, along with the leaders of Shechem who helped him murder them. **9:25** The leaders of Shechem rebelled against Abimelech by putting bandits in the hills, who robbed everyone who traveled by on the road. But Abimelech found out about it.

9:26 Gaal son of Ebed came through Shechem with his brothers. The leaders of Shechem transferred their loyalty to him. **9:27** They went out to the field, harvested their grapes, squeezed out the juice, and celebrated. They came to the temple of their god and ate, drank, and cursed Abimelech. **9:28** Gaal son of Ebed said, "Who is Abimelech and who is Shechem, that we should serve him? Is he not the son of Jerub-Baal, and is not Zebul the deputy he appointed? Serve the sons of Hamor, the father of Shechem! But why should we serve Abimelech? **9:29** If only these men were under my command, I would get rid of Abimelech!" He challenged Abimelech, "Muster your army and come out for battle!"

9:30 When Zebul, the city commissioner, heard the words of Gaal son of Ebed, he was furious. **9:31** He sent messengers to Abimelech, who was in Arumah, reporting, "Beware! Gaal son of Ebed and his brothers are coming to Shechem and inciting the city to rebel against you. **9:32** Now, come up at night with your men and set an ambush in the field outside the city. **9:33** In the morning at sunrise quickly attack the city. When he and his men come out to fight you, do what you can to him."

9:34 So Abimelech and all his men came up at night and set an ambush outside Shechem—they divided into four units. **9:35** When Gaal son of Ebed came out and stood at the entrance to the city's gate, Abimelech and his men got up from their hiding places. **9:36** Gaal saw the men and said to Zebul, "Look, men are coming down from the tops of the hills." But Zebul said to him, "You are seeing the shadows on the hills—it just looks like men." **9:37** Gaal again said, "Look, men are coming down from the very center of the land. A unit is coming by way of the Oak Tree of the Diviners. **9:38** Zebul said to him, "Where now are your bragging words, 'Who is Abimelech that we should serve him?' Are these not the men you insulted? Go out now and fight them!" **9:39** So Gaal led the leaders of Shechem out and fought Abimelech. **9:40** Abimelech chased him, and Gaal ran from him. Many Shechemites fell wounded at the opening of the gate. **9:41** Abimelech went back to Arumah; Zebul drove Gaal and his brothers out of Shechem.

9:42 The next day the Shechemites came out to the field. When Abimelech heard about it, **9:43** he took his men and divided them into three units and set an ambush in the field. When he saw the people coming out of the city, he attacked and struck them down. **9:44** Abimelech and his units attacked and blocked the entrance to the city's gate. Two units then attacked all the people in the field and struck them down. **9:45** Abimelech fought against the city all that day. He captured the city and killed all the people in it. Then he leveled the city and spread salt over it.

9:46 When all the leaders of the Tower of Shechem heard the news, they went to the stronghold of the temple of El-Berith. **9:47** Abimelech heard that all the leaders of the Tower of Shechem were in one place. **9:48** He and all his men went up on Mount Zalmon. He took an ax in his hand and cut off a tree branch. He put it on his shoulder and said to his men, "Quickly, do what you have just seen me do!" **9:49** So each of his men also cut off a branch and followed Abimelech. They put the branches against the stronghold and set fire to it. All the people of the Tower of Shechem died—about a thousand men and women.

9:50 Abimelech moved on to Thebez; he besieged and captured it. **9:51** There was a fortified tower in the center of the city, so all the men and women, as well as the city's leaders, ran into it and locked the entrance. Then they went up to the roof of the tower. **9:52** Abimelech came and attacked the tower. When he approached the entrance of the tower to set it on fire, **9:53** a woman threw an upper millstone down on his head and shattered his skull. **9:54** He quickly called to the young man who carried his weapons, "Draw your sword and kill me, so they will not say, 'A woman killed him.' So the young man stabbed him and he died. **9:55** When the Israelites saw that Abimelech was dead, they went home.

9:56 God repaid Abimelech for the evil he did to his father by murdering his seventy half-brothers. **9:57** God also repaid the men of Shechem for their evil deeds. The curse spoken by Jotham son of Jerub-Baal fell on them.

Would you say, based on the evidence provided in this section, that Israel was getting closer to or farther from the goal God had for the nation?

_____

_____

2. **Location**—Where was Joshua, Moses' successor, when he drew up the decrees and laws for the people to follow?

> **Joshua 24:25** That day Joshua drew up an agreement for the people, and he established rules and regulations for them in Shechem. **24:26** Joshua wrote these words in the Law Scroll of God. He then took a large stone and set it up there under the oak tree near the Lord's shrine. **24:27** Joshua said to all the people, "Look, this stone will be a witness against you, for it has heard everything the Lord said to us. It will be a witness against you if you deny your God."

_____

3. Read Judges 9:6 below. Where was Abimelech, Gideon's son, when the people crowned him king?

> **Judges 9:6** All the leaders of Shechem and Beth Millo assembled and then went and made Abimelech king by the oak near the pillar in Shechem.

_____

4. Compare the two events and the two locations. What do they suggest about what had happened to the nation spiritually?

_____

_____

_____

_____

5. Jotham, the only surviving son of Gideon whom Abimelech had not killed, went to the top of Mount Gerizim (9:7) and told the people a parable. Gerizim is the same place where six of Israel's tribes had declared the blessings of abiding by God's law.

A. What injustice had Jotham suffered (v. 5)?

_____

_____

B. After Jotham's speech, what did he do (v. 21)? Did he gather an army and avenge his brothers' deaths?

_____

_____

_____

C. Did God avenge the injustices (v. 56)?

_____

_____

D. How did Abimelech die? Was it an honorable death (vv. 53—54)?

_____

_____

6. Up to this point in Judges, after each major section we've seen a repeating phrase (emphasis added in each of the Scripture passages below):

> **3:11 The land had rest** for forty years; then Othniel son of Kenaz died.

> **3:30** Israel humiliated Moab that day, and **the land had rest** for eighty years.

> **5:31** May all your enemies perish like this, O Lord! But may those who love you shine like the rising sun at its brightest!" And **the land had rest** for forty years.

> **8:28** The Israelites humiliated Midian; the Midianites' fighting spirit was broken. **The land had rest** for forty years during Gideon's time.

Why do you suppose we don't see the phrase "the land had rest" again in the Book of Judges after Abimelech?

_____

_____

_____

SATURDAY: COURAGEOUS WARRIOR?

Imagine you're a farmer who has spent the past the year working hard to reap a harvest, only to have it stripped clean by your enemies. That's what had happened to the Israelites eight years running when God raised up Gideon to lead them. Another harvest season had rolled around, and the evil Midianite army sat perched nearby, one hundred thirty-five thousand soldiers strong.

Probably to keep from being spotted, Gideon was working down in a hole, threshing his wheat in a wine press. In short, he was weak and scared. And God came to him, calling him, "courageous warrior."

Who was He kidding?

After Gideon's initial hesitancy, evidenced by his demand that God perform some signs, he rallied the troops to go up against the Midianites. But Israel had inferior weapons, and they were outnumbered by more than one hundred thousand men. God had Gideon right where He wanted him.

While Gideon was trembling in his boots over the size of his own tiny army, God surprised him by saying, "You have too many men for Me to deliver Midian into your hands."

Too many? Again, He must be kidding.

Why would He say that? "In order that Israel may not boast against me that her own strength has saved her" (7:2).

We're not much different, are we? We get scared about something. Then once God works through us to do something amazing, we think we're hot stuff. And in our arrogance and credit-taking, we miss the good stuff. We fail to see that we're never too small or too weak for God to use, but we *can* be too big and too strong.

God had Gideon trim down the ranks of his men until the Israelite army was outnumbered thirteen to one. But that was *still* too strong.

Finally, God had Gideon hang on to the soldiers who brought water to their mouths to drink. The soldiers who drank by kneeling were sent home. Perhaps those who brought water to their mouths were too fearful and wary to take their eyes off the enemy. So Gideon kept three hundred of them. That was his entire army: three hundred scaredy-cats against one hundred fifty thousand. The odds? Four hundred fifty to one.

As if the numbers weren't bad enough, the weapons needed to be pathetic for God to make His point. So when it was time to hand them out, Gideon gave no one spears. There weren't even any ox goads or tent pegs. Just jars, horns, and torches. Some weapons!

Gideon must have been scratching his head wondering how God was going to pull off this victory. But then he overheard one of the enemy talking about a dream in which they (the enemy) were defeated. Suddenly he understood God's "new math": God + Gideon = a majority. And Gideon worshiped (7:15). Gideon finally got it. Now he was ready for battle.

It was night when Gideon gave the command. So his men waved torches, smashed jars, and blew horns. There was lots of clamor and confusion, and in the insanity of it all, the enemy turned on their own ranks and slaughtered each other. Gideon's men didn't even have to fight.

Is there any doubt about where the victory came from? We can never be too weak, but we *can* be too strong. The battle is the Lord's. We do not fight alone.

We're not ready for battle until we've worshiped.

Does it ever bother you that you're weak? Do you compare yourself to others and come up short? Do you have limitations such as poor health, an unimpressive résumé, lack of talent, few connections, average features, weight struggles, or fewer brains than others? Do you feel too afraid to tell others about what a great change the Lord has brought in your life? God is bigger than any obstacle you face.

Once you recognize your weakness and worship, God has you right where He wants you. You're in a perfect position for Him to show His power in such a way that there's no doubt who won the battle.

No kidding.

If there's one thing we can learn from Gideon it's that God can do great works through a reluctant servant suffering from insecurity.

Hail, courageous warrior!

Prayer: *Heavenly Father, Thank You that You're a big, big God. Thank You that You can take the very areas where I'm weak and have failed and can use those very weaknesses for Your own glory. Help me to remember that while the rest of the world tends to focus on what's seen, You look at the heart. Help me to be humble before You, ready to instantly obey Your Spirit's promptings. Help me to see that with You helping me, I always have a majority. Show Your perfect power in my weakness, and help me remember always to give You the glory. In Jesus' name I pray. Amen.*

For Memorization: "The Lord's messenger appeared and said to him, 'The Lord is with you, courageous warrior!' " (Judg. 6:12)

WEEK 4 OF 6

Jephthah: Judges 10—12

SUNDAY: THE CHIEF DONKEY-RIDER

Scripture: "After him Abdon son of Hillel the Pirathonite led Israel. He had forty sons and thirty grandsons who rode on seventy donkeys." (Judg. 12:13–14)

Remember Achsa, Caleb's daughter? Back in the first chapter of Judges we read that "When she got off her donkey, Caleb asked her, 'What would you like?'" (Judges 1:14). Now, why do you suppose the author wanted us to know she was on a donkey?

Chapter one isn't the only place in Judges where a donkey is mentioned. Deborah and Barak sang, "You who ride on light-colored female donkeys, who sit on saddle cloths . . . you who walk on the road, pay attention!" (5:10).

Later we read "[Jair] had thirty sons who rode on thirty donkeys, and they possessed thirty cities. To this day these towns are called Havvoth Jair—they are in the land of Gildead" (Judges 10:3–4).

Two chapters later, we read that Abdon son of Hillel, from Pirathon, led Israel. He had forty sons and thirty grandsons who rode on seventy donkeys (Judg. 12:13–14).

In 1 Samuel we read that rich woman Abigail came riding her donkey as she approached King David (1 Sam. 25:20).

Seeing a pattern yet? Today on *Lifestyles of the Rich and Famous* we expect to see Rolls Royces. But in the garages of the rich and famous back in the ancient Near East, we would have found donkeys. Consider the following narrative, in which King David speaks to his wife, Bathsheba, about their son:

> "I will keep today the oath I swore to you by the Lord God of Israel: 'Surely Solomon your son will be king after me; he will sit in my place on my throne.'" Bathsheba bowed down to the king with her face to the floor and said, "May my master, King David, live forever!"
>
> King David said, "Summon Zadok the priest, Nathan the prophet, and Benaiah son of Jehoiada." They came before the king, and he told them, "Take your master's servants with you, put my son Solomon on my mule, and lead him down to Gihon. There Zadok the priest and Nathan the prophet will anoint him king over Israel; then blow the trumpet and declare, 'Long live King Solomon!'" (1 Kgs. 1:30–34)

A coronation required a mule—the king's own mule. Beasts of burden, not fine horses, were the transportation of the nobility.

Solomon, on his coronation day, rode his father's mule as he made his grand entry into the capital city. Keep that image in mind as you read this prophecy about the Messiah:

> Rejoice greatly, daughter of Zion! Shout, daughter of Jerusalem! Look! Your king is coming to you; he is legitimate and victorious, humble and riding on a donkey—on a young donkey, colt, the foal of a female donkey. I will remove the chariots from Ephraim and the warhorse from Jerusalem, and the battle bow will be removed. Then he will announce peace to the nations. His dominion will be from sea to sea and from the Euphrates River to the ends of the earth. (Zech. 9:9–10)

Does this bring an image to mind? Do you know the day this prophecy was initially fulfilled? Today we commemorate it on Palm Sunday— one week before Easter.

Do you see the significance of Jesus' riding a donkey during His triumphal entry? He entered Jerusalem similarly to how Solomon entered the city on his own coronation day. And the people called Jesus the King of Israel. John records it this way in his Gospel:

The next day the large crowd that had come to the feast heard that Jesus was coming to Jerusalem. So they took branches of palm trees and went out to meet him. They began to shout, **"Hosanna! Blessed is the one who comes in the name of the Lord!** Blessed is the king of Israel!"

Jesus found a young donkey and sat on it, just as it is written, "Do not be afraid, O people of Zion; look, your king is coming, seated on a donkey's colt!"

(His disciples did not understand these things when they first happened, but when Jesus was glorified, then they remembered these things were written about him and that these thingshappened to him.) (John 12:12–16, emphasis added)

The people called Jesus the "King of Israel"! Their king had arrived, righteous and bringing salvation, gentle and riding on a donkey's colt.

When we breeze through the history portions of the Bible, it's easy to miss the significance of some of the details. Who would guess Achsa's riding a donkey or the sons of the judges riding around on donkeys would provide clues to help us understand something about Jesus? Like the disciples, we may see many things only in retrospect as we look back and examine the whole story.

In His second advent, our King will arrive on a white horse ready to make war and avenge those who have persecuted His Bride. But in His first advent, Jesus entered the Holy City in like manner as His ancestor and His nations' leaders before Him—the King of Kings on a donkey, seated on a donkey's colt, announcing peace.

MONDAY: OVERVIEW

1. Read Judges 10–12 after praying for insight.

Judges 10
Stability Restored

10:1 After Abimelech's death, Tola son of Puah, grandson of Dodo, from the tribe of Issachar, rose up to deliver Israel. He lived in Shamir in the Ephraimite hill country. **10:2** He led Israel for twenty-three years, then died and was buried in Shamir.

10:3 Jair the Gileadite rose up after him; he led Israel for twenty-two years. **10:4** He had thirty sons who rode on thirty donkeys and possessed thirty cities. To this day these towns are called Havvoth Jair—they are in the land of Gilead. **10:5** Jair died and was buried in Kamon.

10:6 The Israelites again did evil in the Lord's sight. They worshiped the Baals and the Ashtars, as well as the gods of Syria, Sidon, Moab, the Ammonites, and the Philistines. They abandoned the Lord and did not worship him. **10:7** The Lord was furious with Israel and turned them over to the Philistines and Ammonites. **10:8** They ruthlessly oppressed the Israelites that eighteenth year—that is, all the Israelites living east of the Jordan in Amorite country in Gilead. **10:9** The Ammonites crossed the Jordan to fight with Judah, Benjamin, and Ephraim. Israel suffered greatly.

10:10 The Israelites cried out for help to the Lord: "We have sinned against you. We abandoned our God and worshiped the Baals." **10:11** The Lord said to the Israelites, "Did I not deliver you from Egypt, the Amorites, the Ammonites, the Philistines, **10:12** the Sidonians, Amalek, and Midian when they oppressed you? You cried out for help to me, and I delivered you from their power. **10:13** But since you abandoned me and worshiped other gods, I will not deliver you again. **10:14** Go and cry for help to the gods you have chosen! Let them deliver you from trouble!" **10:15** But the Israelites said to the Lord, "We have sinned. You do to us as you see fit, but deliver us today!" **10:16** They threw away the foreign gods they owned and worshiped the Lord. Finally the Lord became tired of seeing Israel suffer so much.

10:17 The Ammonites assembled and camped in Gilead; the Israelites gathered together and camped in Mizpah. **10:18** The leaders of Gilead said to one another, "Who is willing to lead the charge against the Ammonites? He will become the leader of all who live in Gilead!"

Judges 11

11:1 Now Jephthah the Gileadite was a brave warrior. His mother was a prostitute, but Gilead was his father. **11:2** Gilead's wife also gave him sons. When his wife's sons grew up, they made Jephthah leave and said to him, "You are not going to inherit any of our father's wealth, because you are another woman's son." **11:3** So Jephthah left his half-brothers and lived in the land of Tob. Lawless men joined Jephthah's gang and traveled with him.

11:4 It was some time after this when the Ammonites fought with Israel. **11:5** When the Ammonites attacked, the leaders of Gilead asked Jephthah to come back from the land of Tob. **11:6** They said, "Come, be our commander, so we can fight with the Ammonites." **11:7** Jephthah said to the leaders of Gilead, "But you hated me and made me leave my father's house. Why do you come to me now, when you are in trouble?" **11:8** The leaders of Gilead said to Jephthah, "That may be true, but now we pledge to you our loyalty. Come with us and fight with the Ammonites. Then you will become the leader of all who live in Gilead." **11:9** Jephthah said to the leaders of Gilead, "All right! If you take me back to fight with the Ammonites and the Lord gives them to me, I will be your leader." **11:10** The leaders of Gilead said to Jephthah, "The Lord will judge any grievance you have against us, if we do not do as you say." **11:11** So Jephthah went with the leaders of Gilead. The people made him their leader and commander. Jephthah repeated the terms of the agreement before the Lord in Mizpah.

11:12 Jephthah sent messengers to the Ammonite king, saying, "Why have you come against me to attack my land?" **11:13** The Ammonite king said to Jephthah's messengers, "Because Israel stole my land when they came up from Egypt—from the Arnon River in the south to the Jabbok River in the north, and as far west as the Jordan. Now return it peaceably!"

11:14 Jephthah sent messengers back to the Ammonite king **11:15** and said to him, "This is what Jephthah says, 'Israel did not steal the land of Moab and the land of the Ammonites. **11:16** When they left Egypt, Israel traveled through the desert as far as the Red Sea and then came to Kadesh. **11:17** Israel sent messengers to the king of Edom, saying, "Please allow us to pass through your land." But the king of Edom rejected the request. Israel sent the same request to the king of Moab, but he was unwilling to cooperate. So Israel stayed at Kadesh. **11:18** Then Israel went through the desert and bypassed the land of Edom and the land of Moab. They traveled east of the land of Moab and camped on the other side of the Arnon River; they did not go through Moabite territory (the Arnon was Moab's border). **11:19** Israel sent messengers to King Sihon, the Amorite king who ruled in Heshbon, and said to him, "Please allow us to pass through your land to our land." **11:20** But Sihon did not trust Israel to pass through his territory. He assembled his whole army, camped in Jahaz, and fought with Israel. **11:21** The Lord God of Israel handed Sihon and his whole army over to Israel and they defeated them. Israel took all the land of the Amorites who lived in that land. **11:22** They took all the Amorite territory from the Arnon River on the south to the Jabbok River on the north, from the desert in the east to the Jordan in the west. **11:23** Since the Lord God of Israel has driven out the Amorites before his people Israel, do you think you can just take it from them? **11:24** You have the right to take what Chemosh your god gives you, but we will take the land of all whom the Lord our God has driven out before us. **11:25** Are you really better than Balak son of Zippor, king of Moab? Did he dare to quarrel with Israel? Did he dare to fight with them? **11:26** Israel has been living in Heshbon and its nearby towns, in Aroer and its nearby towns, and in all the cities along the Arnon for three hundred years! Why did you not reclaim them during that time? **11:27** I have not done you wrong, but you are doing wrong by attacking me. May the Lord, the Judge, judge this day between the Israelites and the Ammonites!'" **11:28** But the Ammonite king disregarded the message sent by Jephthah.

11:29 The Lord's spirit empowered Jephthah. He passed through Gilead and Manasseh and went to Mizpah in Gilead. From there he approached the Ammonites. **11:30** Jephthah made a vow to the Lord, saying, "If you really do hand the Ammonites over to me, **11:31** then whoever is the first to come through the doors of my house to meet me when I return safely from fighting the Ammonites—he will belong to the Lord and I will offer him up as a burnt sacrifice." **11:32** Jephthah approached the Ammonites to fight with them, and the Lord handed them over to him. **11:33** He defeated them from Aroer all the way to Minnith—twenty cities in all, even as far as Abel Keramim! He wiped them out! The Israelites humiliated the Ammonites.

11:34 When Jephthah came home to Mizpah, there was his daughter coming out to meet him, dancing to the rhythm of tambourines. She was his only child; except for her he had no son or daughter. **11:35** When he saw her, he ripped his clothes and said, "Oh no! My daughter! You have completely ruined me! You have brought me disaster! I made an oath to the Lord, and I cannot break it." **11:36** She said to him, "My father, since you made an oath to the Lord, do to me as you promised. After all, the Lord vindicated you before your enemies, the Ammonites." **11:37** She then said to her father, "Please grant me this one wish. For two months allow me to walk through the hills with my friends and mourn my virginity." **11:38** He said, "You may go." He permitted her to leave for two months. She went with her friends and mourned her virginity as she walked through the hills. **11:39** After two months she returned to her father, and he did to her as he had vowed. She died a virgin. Her tragic death gave rise to a custom in Israel. **11:40** Every year Israelite women commemorate the daughter of Jephthah the Gileadite for four days.

Judges 12

12:1 The Ephraimites assembled and crossed over to Zaphon. They said to Jephthah, "Why did you go and fight with the Ammonites without asking us to go with you? We will burn your house down right over you." **12:2** Jephthah said to them, "My people and I were entangled in controversy with the Ammonites. I asked for your help, but you did not deliver me from their power. **12:3** When I saw that you were not going to help, I risked my life and advanced against the Ammonites, and the Lord handed them over to me. Why have you come up to fight with me today?" **12:4** Jephthah assembled all the men of Gilead and they fought with Ephraim. The men of Gilead defeated Ephraim, because the Ephraimites insulted them, saying, "You Gileadites are refugees in Ephraim, living within Ephraim's and Manasseh's territory." **12:5** The Gileadites captured the fords of the Jordan River opposite Ephraim. Whenever an Ephraimite fugitive said, "Let me cross over," the men of Gilead asked him, "Are you an Ephraimite?" If he said, "No," **12:6** then they said to him, "Say 'Shibboleth.'" If he said, "Sibboleth," and could not pronounce the word correctly, they grabbed him and executed him right there at the fords of the Jordan. On that day forty-two thousand Ephraimites fell dead. **12:7** Jephthah led Israel for six years; then he died and was buried in his city in Gilead.

12:8 After him Ibzan of Bethlehem led Israel. **12:9** He had thirty sons. He arranged for thirty of his daughters to be married outside his extended family, and he arranged for thirty young women to be brought from outside as wives for his sons. Ibzan led Israel for seven years; **12:10** then he died and was buried in Bethlehem.

12:11 After him Elon the Zebulunite led Israel for ten years. **12:12** Then Elon the Zebulunite died and was buried in Aijalon in the land of Zebulun.

12:13 After him Abdon son of Hillel the Pirathonite led Israel. **12:14** He had forty sons and thirty grandsons who rode on seventy donkeys. He led Israel for eight years. **12:15** Then Abdon son of Hillel the Pirathonite died and was buried in Pirathon in the land of Ephraim, in the hill country of the Amalekites.

2. Write any observations and questions you may have.

_____

_____

_____

_____

TUESDAY: A MAN WITH A PAST

1. Re-read Judges 10:6–18.

> **Judges 10:6** The Israelites again did evil in the Lord's sight. They worshiped the Baals and the Ashtars, as well as the gods of Syria, Sidon, Moab, the Ammonites, and the Philistines. They abandoned the Lord and did not worship him. **10:7** The Lord was furious with Israel and turned them over to the Philistines and Ammonites. **10:8** They ruthlessly oppressed the Israelites that eighteenth year—that is, all the Israelites living east of the Jordan in Amorite country in Gilead. **10:9** The Ammonites crossed the Jordan to fight with Judah, Benjamin, and Ephraim. Israel suffered greatly.
>
> **10:10** The Israelites cried out for help to the Lord: "We have sinned against you. We abandoned our God and worshiped the Baals." **10:11** The Lord said to the Israelites, "Did I not deliver you from Egypt, the Amorites, the Ammonites, the Philistines, **10:12** the Sidonians, Amalek, and Midian when they oppressed you? You cried out for help to me, and I delivered you from their power. **10:13** But since you abandoned me and worshiped other gods, I will not deliver you again. **10:14** Go and cry for help to the gods you have chosen! Let them deliver you from trouble!" **10:15** But the Israelites said to the Lord, "We have sinned. You do to us as you see fit, but deliver us today!" **10:16** They threw away the foreign gods they owned and worshiped the Lord. Finally the Lord became tired of seeing Israel suffer so much.
>
> **10:17** The Ammonites assembled and camped in Gilead; the Israelites gathered together and camped in Mizpah. **10:18** The leaders of Gilead said to one another, "Who is willing to lead the charge against the Ammonites? He will become the leader of all who live in Gilead!"

What parts of the cycle (sin, suffering, supplication, salvation) begin this story? Note that the confession "We have sinned" occurs only two times in the entire book of Judges—both times in this chapter (verses 10, 15).

_____

_____

_____

_____

2. How does prayer factor into God's actions?

_____

_____

_____

3. God raised up Jephthah in response to the prayers of His people for deliverance. Take a few moments to plead with God on behalf His people—the persecuted church, the church worldwide, and your own church. Remember that prayer is a powerful way to influence one's culture.

4. What does this section of Scripture suggest about God's character?

_____

_____

_____

_____

5. Read Judges 11:1–11.

> **Judges 11:1** Now Jephthah the Gileadite was a brave warrior. His mother was a prostitute, but Gilead was his father. **11:2** Gilead's wife also gave him sons. When his wife's sons grew up, they made

Jephthah leave and said to him, "You are not going to inherit any of our father's wealth, because you are another woman's son." **11:3** So Jephthah left his half-brothers and lived in the land of Tob. Lawless men joined Jephthah's gang and traveled with him.

11:4 It was some time after this when the Ammonites fought with Israel. **11:5** When the Ammonites attacked, the leaders of Gilead asked Jephthah to come back from the land of Tob. **11:6** They said, "Come, be our commander, so we can fight with the Ammonites." **11:7** Jephthah said to the leaders of Gilead, "But you hated me and made me leave my father's house. Why do you come to me now, when you are in trouble?" **11:8** The leaders of Gilead said to Jephthah, "That may be true, but now we pledge to you our loyalty. Come with us and fight with the Ammonites. Then you will become the leader of all who live in Gilead." **11:9** Jephthah said to the leaders of Gilead, "All right! If you take me back to fight with the Ammonites and the Lord gives them to me, I will be your leader." **11:10** The leaders of Gilead said to Jephthah, "The Lord will judge any grievance you have against us, if we do not do as you say." **11:11** So Jephthah went with the leaders of Gilead. The people made him their leader and commander. Jephthah repeated the terms of the agreemen before the Lord in Mizpah.

In your own words describe Jephthah's family background.

_____

_____

_____

_____

6. Jephthah didn't use his rough background as an excuse for a victim mentality or a reason to justify disobeying God. Is there anything in your past that you're using as an excuse to avoid totally following God? If so, what? Spend some time praying for yourself or for others you know who are letting the past dictate the present and future.

_____

_____

WEDNESDAY: THE DIPLOMAT

1. Re-read 11:12–28.

11:12 Jephthah sent messengers to the Ammonite king, saying, "Why have you come against me to attack my land?" **11:13** The Ammonite king said to Jephthah's messengers, "Because Israel stole my land when they came up from Egypt—from the Arnon River in the south to the Jabbok River in the north, and as far west as the Jordan. Now return it peaceably!"

11:14 Jephthah sent messengers back to the Ammonite king **11:15** and said to him, "This is what Jephthah says, 'Israel did not steal the land of Moab and the land of the Ammonites. **11:16** When they left Egypt, Israel traveled through the desert as far as the Red Sea and then came to Kadesh. **11:17** Israel sent messengers to the king of Edom, saying, "Please allow us to pass through your land." But the king of Edom rejected the request. Israel sent the same request to the king of Moab, but he was unwilling to cooperate. So Israel stayed at Kadesh. **11:18** Then Israel went through the desert and bypassed the land of Edom and the land of Moab. They traveled east of the land of Moab and camped on the other side of the Arnon River; they did not go through Moabite territory (the Arnon was Moab's border). **11:19** Israel sent messengers to King Sihon, the Amorite king who ruled in Heshbon, and said to him, "Please allow us to pass through your land to our land." **11:20** But Sihon did not trust Israel to pass through his territory. He assembled his whole army, camped in Jahaz, and fought with Israel. **11:21** The Lord God of Israel handed Sihon and his whole army over to Israel and they defeated them. Israel took all the land of the Amorites who lived in that land. **11:22** They took all the Amorite territory from the Arnon River on the south to the Jabbok River on the north, from the desert in the east to the Jordan in the west. **11:23** Since the Lord God of Israel has driven out the Amorites before his people Israel, do you think you can just take it from them? **11:24** You have the right to take what Chemosh your god gives you, but we will take the land of all whom the Lord our God has driven out before us. **11:25** Are you really better than Balak son of Zippor, king of Moab?

Did he dare to quarrel with Israel? Did he dare to fight with them? **11:26** Israel has been living in Heshbon and its nearby towns, in Aroer and its nearby towns, and in all the cities along the Arnon for three hundred years! Why did you not reclaim them during that time? **11:27** I have not done you wrong, but you are doing wrong by attacking me. May the Lord, the Judge, judge this day between the Israelites and the Ammonites!' " **11:28** But the Ammonite king disregarded the message sent by Jephthah.

What is the political situation as described in this passage?

_____

_____

_____

2. We might expect Jephthah to strike first and negotiate later, but instead he initiates peace talks and gives his opponents three lessons:

- **A lesson in history.** Jephthah tells them, in effect, "We captured the land from the Amorites, not Ammonites." Ammon had no right to the land east of the Jordan they were trying to obtain by force. Jephthah traces the history of how this territory came into Israel's possession. Israel had not attacked any territory held by Ammon or Moab when God's people approached the Promised Land in Moses' day. Israel had taken the land in a dispute from the Amorites, who had previously captured it from the Ammonites.

- **A theology lesson.** "The Lord gave us this land." That in itself could have been the last word. Even pagans recognized that when victory was given by a deity, the victors had a right to possess that territory. Powerful King Balak of Moab had never fought with Israel, because he realized it would be futile to fight Israel's God.

- **A logic lesson.** "For three hundred years we have had it and you have not fussed. Why didn't you speak up earlier?"

How does the king of Ammon respond (v. 28)?

_____

_____

3. By looking up the references listed below, note what similarities you see between how Israel treats God (ch. 10) and how Gilead treats Jephthah?

How did Israel treat God?   How did Gilead treat Jephthah?

10:6	11:1–3
10:7–9	11:4
10:10	11:5–6
10:11–14	11:7
10:15–16	11:8
10:16	11:9–11

THURSDAY: JEPHTHAH'S VOW

1. Flip back to the excerpts of Judges 11 found on pages 80–82. What is God's involvement in Jephthah's story (see 11:29)?

_____

_____

2. What does Jephthah vow (see 11:30–31)?

_____

_____

_____

_____

> The wording of Jephthah's vow could be translated "Either it shall be the Lord's or I shall offer it for a burnt offering."

3. Re-read Judges 11:32–40.

> **Judges 11:32** Jephthah approached the Ammonites to fight with them, and the Lord handed them over to him. **11:33** He defeated them from Aroer all the way to Minnith—twenty cities in all, even as far as Abel Keramim! He wiped them out! The Israelites humiliated the Ammonites.
>
> **11:34** When Jephthah came home to Mizpah, there was his

daughter coming out to meet him, dancing to the rhythm of tambourines. She was his only child; except for her he had no son or daughter. **11:35** When he saw her, he ripped his clothes and said, "Oh no! My daughter! You have completely ruined me! You have brought me disaster! I made an oath to the Lord, and I cannot break it." **11:36** She said to him, "My father, since you made an oath to the Lord, do to me as you promised. After all, the Lord vindicated you before your enemies, the Ammonites." **11:37** She then said to her father, "Please grant me this one wish. For two months allow me to walk through the hills with my friends and mourn my virginity." **11:38** He said, "You may go." He permitted her to leave for two months. She went with her friends and mourned her virginity as she walked through the hills. **11:39** After two months she returned to her father, and he did to her as he had vowed. She died a virgin. Her tragic death gave rise to a custom in Israel. **11:40** Every year Israelite women commemorate the daughter of Jephthah the Gileadite for four days.

Describe in your own words what has happened here.

Many believe Jephthah engaged in child sacrifice; others believe his daughter was set apart for the Lord, which required her to remain a virgin for life. Today single women make up an enormous percentage of the population, so the idea of remaining unmarried is pretty normal in our world. But at the time of Judges, growing up and remaining single would have been a tragedy for both father and daughter. Women were illiterate and had almost no way of earning money to support themselves. They depended on husbands and children to be their nursing homes, their retirement plans, their protection, and their security. Similarly, an old man with no sons to protect him and buy his food was truly vulnerable.

4. Regardless of whether Jephthah's daughter was sacrificed or lived but remained a virgin, she was his only child, so he was left without an heir as a result of his vow. It cost them both a lot for him to keep his vow to the Lord. What did his daughter bewail? (See 11:38–39 below.)

> **Judges 11:38** He said, "You may go." He permitted her to leave for two months. She went with her friends and mourned her virginity as she walked through the hills. **11:39** After two months she returned to her father, and he did to her as he had vowed. She died a virgin. Her tragic death gave rise to a custom in Israel. **11:40** Every year Israelite women commemorate the daughter of Jephthah the Gileadite for four days.

---

5. Jephthah kept his vow to God at great personal sacrifice. Are you making easy promises to God and others and then failing to keep them? Does your "yes" mean "yes," or does it mean "maybe"? List things you've said you would do and determine now to keep your word.

---

6. What was Jephthah's daughter doing when she came out to meet him after his successful battle?

> **Judges 11:34** When Jephthah came home to Mizpah, there was his daughter coming out to meet him, dancing to the rhythm of tambourines (Judges 11:34).

---

7. What do you see women doing after a battle victory in each of the following passages?

Exodus 15:20–21 Then Miriam the prophetess, the sister of Aaron, took a hand-drum in her hand, and all the women went out after her with hand-drums and with dances. And Miriam sang in response to them, "Sing to the Lord, for he has triumphed gloriously; the horse and its rider he has thrown into the sea."

1 Samuel 18:6 When the men arrived after David returned from striking down the Philistine, the women from all the cities of Israel came out singing and dancing to meet King Saul. They were happy as they played their tambourines and three-stringed instruments.

Jeremiah 31:4 I will rebuild you, my dear children, Israel, so that you will once again be built up. Once again you will take up the tambourine and join in the happy throng of dancers.

_____

_____

_____

8. Women customarily greeted the returning warriors of their community with dancing, singing, tambourines, and music. They led the people in praising God. Today, God does not call us to defend a physical nation of His chosen people, but we do engage in spiritual warfare. Do you make praise and celebration of God's victories part of your work?

_____

_____

_____

_____

FRIDAY: CIVIL WAR

1. Re-read Judges 12:1–7.

Judges 12:1 The Ephraimites assembled and crossed over to Zaphon. They said to Jephthah, "Why did you go and fight with the Ammonites without asking us to go with you? We will burn your house down right over you." **12:2** Jephthah said to them, "My people and I were entangled in controversy with the Ammonites. I asked for your help, but you did not deliver me from their power. **12:3** When I saw that you were not going to help, I risked my life and advanced against the Ammonites, and the Lord handed them over to me. Why have you come up to fight with me today?" **12:4** Jephthah assembled all the men of Gilead and they fought with Ephraim. The men of Gilead defeated Ephraim, because the Ephraimites insulted them, saying, "You Gileadites are refugees in Ephraim, living within Ephraim's and Manasseh's territory." **12:5** The Gileadites captured the fords of the Jordan River opposite Ephraim. Whenever an Ephraimite fugitive said, "Let me cross over," the men of Gilead asked him, "Are you an Ephraimite?" If he said, "No," **12:6** then they said to him, "Say 'Shibboleth.'" If he said, "Sibboleth," and could not pronounce the word correctly, they grabbed him and executed him right there at the fords of the Jordan. On that day forty-two thousand Ephraimites fell dead. **12:7** Jephthah led Israel for six years; then he died and was buried in his city in Gilead.

2. Compare the preceding scripture with Judges 8:1–3 in the Gideon account (below).

> **Judges 8:1** The Ephraimites said to him, "Why have you done such a thing to us? You did not summon us when you went to fight the Midianites!" They argued vehemently with him. **8:2** He said to them, "Now what have I accomplished compared to you? Even Ephraim's leftover grapes are better quality than Abiezer's harvest! **8:3** It was to you that God handed over the Midianite generals, Oreb and Zeeb! What did I accomplish to rival that?" When he said this, they calmed down.

Do you see a pattern in the Ephraimites? If so, what?

_____

_____

_____

_____

3. Their whole argument is absurd. For eighteen years the Ammonites overran Gilead, and the tribe of Ephraim ignored their brothers' needs. Now that the battle is over, they're threatening to burn Jephthah alive

for not including them in battle. How obnoxious! Having missed out on the glory, they now want a piece of the reward. *Ephraim is always brave after the battle.* An arrogant, critical, envious group, they're sure of their own rights but are unwilling to accept responsibility. They're willing to fight their own brothers but never the enemy. Jephthah gently points out that they were invited but didn't show up. They sneer at this, so Jephthah and his men turn in fury on them. What is the end result when people want benefits but let everybody else do the work?

_____

_____

_____

_____

_____

4. The nation was called to work *together* to drive out the *enemy*. How would you say they're doing at working together? At driving out the enemy?

_____

_____

_____

_____

_____

5. Do you see God's people acting this way today?

_____

_____

_____

Scripture: Gilead's wife also gave him sons. When his wife's sons grew up, they made Jephthah leave and said to him, "You are not going to inherit any of our father's wealth, because you are another woman's son." (Judges 11:2)

It's a classic Cinderfella story—actually, worse in the beginning. A man "knows" a prostitute in the biblical sense and she conceives and bears a son. That son grows up around his ugly half-brothers, always the outcast. Mom's got a bad "rep," Dad's immoral, and the half-brothers hate him. Sounds like the kind of kid who'll end up singing the Folsom Prison blues.

The "legitimate" sons tell him he can forget it if he thinks he'll ever inherit anything of his daddy's. So all alone in the world, our fella leaves this pathetic loveless family and strikes out on his own. All by himself he goes to a new land.

Somewhere along the way the fear of God enters his thinking.

In the new land he makes some friends. Pretty soon he emerges as somewhat of a local hero. A group of adventurers follow him as if he's the first Robin Hood. The merry men of Tob form a military band that serves as sort of an unofficial police force.

Not long after that, the guys from the old 'hood hear about his success. They arrive saying they want in on the action. They ask Jephthah to help them fight the enemy—which he does, because apparently he doesn't hold a grudge.

"Jephthah was a valiant warrior," writes Gary Inrig in his book *Hearts of Iron, Feet of Clay.* "Because of his tragic family life, he had to become strong to survive. The story of his life is of God taking a strong man, and, by His Spirit, turning him into a usable man. Whatever our strengths and weaknesses, the secret of our usefulness is our availability to our God."[4]

Indeed, the prostitute's son ends up using the name of the Lord more frequently than any other person in Judges. And he recognizes that the battles he fights are God's.

What an unlikely hero!

Some say Jephthah made a rash vow. I'm not sure that's how we're supposed to see it. Shortly before he makes the vow, we read that the Lord came upon him. Maybe he was supposed to make that hard vow

[4] Gary Inrig, *Hearts of Iron, Feet of Clay* (Chicago: Moody Bible Institute, 1979), 89.

and keep it, because he served a God who was more important to him than physical progeny.

Consider Jephthah's family background when you think about what it cost him to keep his word to the Lord. Whether or not he sacrificed his daughter, his vow meant that his lineage ended. His daughter was an only child at a time when families depended on lots of children to carry on the family name and provide for their elders. And Jephthah certainly couldn't fall back on his brothers to feed or protect him in his old age.

In Jephthah's lifetime, he probably thought keeping his word to the Lord had cost him his legacy. But he kept his promise anyway.

In the end, Jephthah didn't really lose out. I'm reminded of God's words in Isaiah:

> **Isaiah 56:4-5** For this is what the Lord says: "For the eunuchs who observe my Sabbaths and choose what pleases me and are faithful to my covenant, I will set up within my temple and my walls a monument that will be better than sons and daughters. I will set up a permanent monument for them that will remain.

Isaiah teaches that those without a physical legacy can leave an even more lasting spiritual legacy. And we see that with Jephthah. Consider this: When we read the names of the faith's great heroes, Jephthah, the man with no sons, is right there on the list in Hebrews 11.

I doubt Jephthah knew about the enduring legacy he left. The Book of Judges had not been written by the time he died. And more than a thousand years passed before Hebrews was composed. Yet even today, two thousand years after that, Jephthah's legacy continues.

What a reversal of circumstances!

We read of similar reversals throughout Scripture, because God specializes in taking the wounded, the broken, the marginalized, the underdog and turning their stories of defeat into stories of victory. Joseph starts out a slave and ends up ruling Egypt. Esther starts out an orphan and ends up the Queen of Persia. David is the youngest of a bunch of brothers who lord it over him and ends up king of Israel. The son of a prostitute ends up in the Faith Hall of Fame. And the greatest reversal of all—an earthquake on a Friday—is followed by a resurrection on Sunday.

God is in the business of turning bad news into good. It's His specialty.

What in your life needs reversing? The effects of a broken family, a broken heart, or broken dreams? All the above? Perhaps your commitment to follow the Lord has cost you dearly.

All He asks is your availability. He can do the rest.

Prayer: *Thank You, Lord, that You're the great God of reversals. Right now I need some reversals in my life. Most of all, I need You to change me and make me like You. But I also need You to take my broken heart, my broken dreams, all the endless longings I have and replace them with Your victory song. Thank You that You are a big God and You know the ending and the beginning that I can't see. Cleanse me, Lord. I yield myself to You, available for your service. Use me to bring glory to You. You are worthy! In Jesus' name I pray. Amen.*

For Memorization: "But the Israelites said to the Lord, 'We have sinned. You do to us as you see fit, but deliver us today!' They threw away the foreign gods they owned and worshiped the Lord. Finally the Lord became tired of seeing Israel suffer so much." (Judg. 10:15–16)

WEEK 5 OF 6

Samson the Conflicted: Judges 13—16

Scripture: "The Lord's angelic messenger appeared to the woman and said to her, 'You are infertile and childless, but you will conceive and have a son.'" (Judges 13:3)

When I ask people to name some of the infertile women in the Bible, they usually rattle off Sarah, Rachel, Hannah, and Elizabeth. But one name virtually never makes the list—Samson's mother. In Judges 13, we find her described as "the wife of Manoah."

As you know from our study so far, the nation of Israel engaged in all sorts of evil acts during the time of the judges. This was certainly true at the time when Manoah and his wife lived. Things were so bad that the Lord had let Israel's enemies conquer them for forty years. The people didn't even cry out to God this time, but He still had mercy.

When it was time for the Lord to intervene, the angel of the Lord came to Manoah's wife with an announcement. He prophesied that she would give birth to a son. That son, he said, was to abstain from alcohol and never shave his head. Then the angel added something of particular importance: "He will begin to deliver Israel from the power of the Philistines" (13:5). What a purpose! That son would be the instrument through whom God would free His people from their oppressors.

Imagine the excitement! Manoah's wife ran to tell her husband what had happened. All those years of infertility were finally punctuated not with another period—but with a pregnancy. Yet in relaying the angel's message to her husband, she left out the most important part—the part about what her son was supposed to become.

Upon hearing the news, Manoah was puzzled. Part of his confusion was probably due to his lack of respect for his wife's testimony—a fairly typical view of women at the time. But she had also left out some important information. So Manoah asked God to send the angel back to tell him more. The angel did so, but when Manoah asked about his son's mode of life and vocation, the angel said this: "Your wife should pay attention to everything I told her" (v. 13).

Manoah's wife was apparently so focused on her temporal good news that she failed to see her own responsibility and the more important spiritual purpose God had in mind.

Notice that the writer of Judges refers to Samson's mother as "Manoah's wife" and "the woman." We are never told her name. This is a significant omission. In biblical times it was very important to have a lasting name. The average person didn't have a family Bible with a family tree listed inside, nor were there cemeteries with lasting headstones. People were remembered when their names were passed down from generation to generation. So when a biblical writer avoided naming someone, as he did with Manoah's wife, it was usually as a signal to the reader that the unnamed character had failed in some way.

For Manoah's wife, the good news about having a baby overshadowed God's more important plans. Having been through infertility myself, I can only imagine how caught up she must have been in the news of her son's conception. What joy she must have felt! Yet in her complete focus on the here and now, she missed the grander picture.

In the story that follows, we see the same focus on the here-and-now in her son, Samson. He had a little problem with immediate gratification. And I can't help wondering if Samson modeled what he saw in his mother.

Do you know your purpose? Do you help others around you find their purpose? Every believer in Jesus Christ has one purpose, and it's clear. It's not about us, and it's not about temporal things. It's—as the Westminster Chatechism so aptly puts it—to glorify God and enjoy Him forever.

How are you doing?

MONDAY: OVERVIEW

After praying for supernatural guidance, read Judges 13—16.

Judges 13

13:1 The Israelites again did evil in the Lord's sight, so the Lord handed them over to the Philistines for forty years.

13:2 There was a man named Manoah from Zorah, from the Danite tribe. His wife was infertile and childless. **13:3** The Lord's angelic messenger appeared to the woman and said to her, "You are infertile and childless, but you will conceive and have a son. **13:4** Now be careful! Do not drink wine or beer, and do not eat any food that will make you ritually unclean. **13:5** Look, you will conceive and have a son. You should not cut his hair, for the child will be dedicated to God from birth. He will begin to deliver Israel from the power of the Philistines."

13:6 The woman went and said to her husband, "A man sent from God came to me! He looked like God's angelic messenger—he was very awesome. I did not ask him where he came from, and he did not tell me his name. **13:7** He said to me, 'Look, you will conceive and have a son. So now, do not drink wine or beer and do not eat any food that will make you ritually unclean. For the child will be dedicated to God from birth till the day he dies.'"

13:8 Manoah prayed to the Lord, "Excuse me, Lord. Please allow the man sent from God to visit us again, so he can teach us how we should raise the child who will be born." **13:9** God answered Manoah's prayer. God's angelic messenger visited the woman again while she was sitting in the field. But her husband Manoah was not with her. **13:10** The woman ran quickly and told her husband, "Come quickly, the man who visited me the other day has appeared to me!" **13:11** So Manoah got up and followed his wife. When he met the man, he said to him, "Are you the man who spoke to this woman?" He said, "Yes." **13:12** Manoah said, "Now, when your announcement comes true, how should the child be raised and what should he do?" **13:13** The Lord's messenger told Manoah, "Your wife should pay attention to everything I told her. **13:14** She should not drink anything that the grapevine produces. She must not drink wine or beer, and she must not eat any food that will make her ritually unclean. She should obey everything I commanded her to do." **13:15** Manoah said to the Lord's messenger, "Please stay here awhile, so we can prepare a young goat for you to eat." **13:16** The Lord's messenger said to Manoah, "If I stay, I will not eat your food. But if you want to make a burnt sacrifice to the Lord, you should offer it." (He said this because Manoah did not know that he was the Lord's messenger.) **13:17** Manoah said to the Lord's messenger, "Tell us your name, so we can honor you when your announcement comes true." **13:18** The Lord's messenger said to him, "You should not ask me my name, because you cannot comprehend it." **13:19** Manoah took a young goat and a grain offering and offered them on a rock to the Lord. The Lord's messenger did an amazing thing as Manoah and his wife watched. **13:20** As the flame went up from the altar toward the sky, the Lord's messenger went up in it while Manoah and his wife watched. They fell facedown to the ground.

13:21 The Lord's messenger did not appear again to Manoah and his wife. After all this happened Manoah realized that the visitor had been the Lord's messenger. **13:22** Manoah said to his wife, "We will certainly die, because we have seen a supernatural being!" **13:23** But his wife said to him, "If the Lord wanted to kill us, he would not have accepted the burnt offering and the grain offering from us. He would not have shown us all these things, or just now have spoken to us like this."

13:24 Manoah's wife gave birth to a son and named him Samson. The child grew and the Lord empowered him. **13:25** The Lord's spirit began to control him in Mahaneh Dan between Zorah and Eshtaol.

Judges 14

14:1 Samson went down to Timnah, where a Philistine girl caught his eye. **14:2** When he got home, he told his father and mother, "A Philistine girl in Timnah has caught my eye. Now get her for my wife." **14:3** But his father and mother said to him, "Certainly you can find a wife among your relatives or among all our people! You should not have to go and get a wife from the uncircumcised Philistines." But Samson said to his father, "Get her for me, because she is the right one for me." **14:4** Now his father and mother did not realize this was the Lord's doing. He was looking for an opportunity to stir up trouble with the Philistines, for at that time the Philistines were ruling Israel.

14:5 Samson went down to Timnah. When he approached the vineyards of Timnah, he saw a roaring young lion attacking him. **14:6** The Lord's spirit empowered him and he tore the lion in two with his bare hands as easily as one would tear a young goat. But he did not tell his father or mother what he had done.

14:7 Samson continued on down to Timnah and spoke to the girl. In his opinion, she was just the right one. **14:8** Some time later, when he went back to marry her, he turned aside to see the lion's remains. He saw a swarm of bees in the lion's carcass, as well as some honey. **14:9** He scooped it up with his hands and ate it as he walked along. When he returned to his father and mother, he offered them some and they ate it. But he did not tell them he had scooped the honey out of the lion's carcass.

14:10 Then Samson's father accompanied him to Timnah for the marriage. Samson hosted a party there, for this was customary for bridegrooms to do. **14:11** When the Philistines saw he had no attendants, they gave him thirty groomsmen who kept him company. **14:12** Samson said to them, "I will give you a riddle. If you really can solve it during the seven days the party lasts, I will give you thirty linen robes and thirty sets of clothes. **14:13** But if you cannot solve it, you will give me thirty linen robes and thirty sets of clothes." They said to him, "Let us hear your riddle." **14:14** He said to them, "Out of the one who eats came something to eat; out of the strong one came something sweet."

They could not solve the riddle for three days.

14:15 On the fourth day they said to Samson's bride, "Trick your husband into giving the solution to the riddle. If you refuse, we will burn up you and your father's family. Did you invite us here to make us poor?" **14:16** So Samson's bride cried on his shoulder and said, "You must hate me; you do not love me! You told the young men a riddle, but you have not told me the solution." He said to her, "Look, I have not even told my father or mother. Do you really expect me to tell you?" **14:17** She cried on his shoulder until the party was almost over. Finally, on the seventh day, he told her because she had nagged him so much. Then she told the young men the solution to the riddle. **14:18** On the seventh day, before the sun set, the men of the city said to him, "What is sweeter than honey? What is stronger than a lion?"

He said to them, "If you had not plowed with my heifer, you would not have solved my riddle!"

14:19 The Lord's spirit empowered him. He went down to Ashkelon and murdered thirty men. He took their clothes and gave them to the men who had solved the riddle. He was furious as he went back home. **14:20** Samson's bride was then given to his best man.

Judges 15

15:1 Sometime later, during the wheat harvest, Samson took a young goat as a gift and went to visit his bride. He said to her father, "I want to have sex with my bride in her bedroom!" But her father would not let him enter. **15:2** Her father said, "I really thought you absolutely despised her, so I gave her to your best man. Her younger sister is more attractive than she is. Take her instead!" **15:3** Samson said to them, "This time I am justified in doing the Philistines harm!" **15:4** Samson went and captured three hundred jackals and got some torches. He tied the jackals in pairs by their tails and then tied a torch to each pair. **15:5** He lit the torches and set the jackals loose in the Philistines' standing grain. He burned up the grain heaps and the standing grain, as well as the vineyards and olive groves. **15:6** The Philistines asked, "Who did this?" They were told, "Samson, the Timnite's son-in-law, because the Timnite took Samson's bride and gave her to his best man." So the Philistines went up and burned her and her father. **15:7** Samson said to them, "Because you did this, I will get revenge against you before I quit fighting." **15:8** He struck them down and defeated them. Then he went down and lived for a time in the cave in the cliff of Etam.

15:9 The Philistines went up and invaded Judah. They arrayed themselves for battle in Lehi. **15:10** The men of Judah said, "Why are you attacking us?" The Philistines said, "We have come up to take Samson prisoner so we can do to him what he has done to us." **15:11** Three thousand men of Judah went down to the cave in the cliff of Etam and said to Samson, "Do you not know that the Philistines rule over us? Why have you done this to us?" He said to them, "I have only done to them what they have done to me." **15:12** They said to him, "We have come down to take you prisoner so we can hand you over to the Philistines." Samson said to them, "Promise me you will not kill me." **15:13** They said to him, "We promise! We will only take you prisoner and hand you over to them. We promise not to kill you." They tied him up with two brand new ropes and led him up from the cliff. **15:14** When he arrived in Lehi, the Philistines shouted as they approached him. But the Lord's spirit empowered him. The ropes around his arms were like flax dissolving in fire, and they melted away from his hands. **15:15** He happened to see a solid jawbone of a donkey. He grabbed it and struck down a thousand men. **15:16** Samson then said,"With the jawbone of a donkey I have left them in heaps; with the jawbone of a donkey I have struck down a thousand men!"

15:17 When he finished speaking, he threw the jawbone down and named that place Ramath Lehi.

15:18 He was very thirsty, so he cried out to the Lord and said, "You have given your servant this great victory. But now must I die of thirst and fall into hands of the Philistines?" **15:19** So God split open the basin at Lehi and water flowed out from it. When he took a drink, his strength was restored and he revived. For this reason he named the spring En Hakkore. It remains in Lehi to this very day. **15:20** Samson led Israel for twenty years during the days of Philistine prominence.

Judges 16

16:1 Samson went to Gaza. There he saw a prostitute and went in to have sex with her. **16:2** The Gazites were told, "Samson has come here!" So they surrounded the town and hid all night at the city gate, waiting for him to leave. They relaxed all night, thinking, "He will not leave until morning comes; then we will kill him!" **16:3** Samson spent half the night with the prostitute; then he got up in the middle of the night and left. He grabbed the doors of the city gate, as well as the two posts, and pulled them right off, bar and all. He put them on his shoulders and carried them up to the top of a hill east of Hebron.

16:4 After this Samson fell in love with a woman named Delilah, who lived in the Sorek Valley. **16:5** The rulers of the Philistines went up to visit her and said to her, "Trick him! Find out what makes him so strong and how we can subdue him and humiliate him. Each one of us will give you eleven hundred silver pieces."

16:6 So Delilah said to Samson, "Tell me what makes you so strong and how you can be subdued and humiliated." **16:7** Samson said to her, "If they tie me up with seven fresh bowstrings that have not been dried, I will become weak and be just like any other man." **16:8** So the rulers of the Philistines brought her seven fresh bowstrings which had not been dried and they tied him up with them. **16:9** They hid in the bedroom and then she said to him, "The Philistines are here, Samson!" He snapped the bowstrings as easily as a thread of yarn snaps when it is put close to fire. The secret of his strength was not discovered.

16:10 Delilah said to Samson, "Look, you deceived me and told me lies. Now tell me how you can be subdued." **16:11** He said to her, "If they tie me tightly with brand new ropes that have never been used, I will become weak and be just like any other man." **16:12** So Delilah took new ropes and tied him with them and said to him, "The Philistines are here, Samson!" (The Philistines were hiding in the bedroom.) But he tore the ropes from his arms as if they were a piece of thread.

16:13 Delilah said to Samson, "Up to now you have deceived me and told me lies. Tell me how you can be subdued." He said to her, "If you weave the seven braids of my hair into the fabric on the loom and secure it with the pin, I will become weak and be like any other man." **16:14** So she made him go to sleep, wove the seven braids of his hair into the fabric on the loom, fastened it with the pin, and said to him, "The Philistines are here, Samson!" He woke up and tore away the pin of the loom and the fabric.

16:15 She said to him, "How can you say, 'I love you,' when you will not share your secret with me? Three times you have deceived me and have not told me what makes you so strong." **16:16** She nagged him every day and pressured him until he was sick to death of it. **16:17** Finally he told her his secret. He said to her, "My hair has never been cut, for I have been dedicated to God from the time I was conceived. If my head were shaved, my strength would leave me; I would become weak, and be just like all other men." **16:18** When Delilah saw that he had told her his secret, she sent for the rulers of the Philistines, saying, "Come up here again, for he has told me his secret. So the rulers of the Philistines went up to visit her, bringing the silver in their hands. **16:19** She made him go to sleep on her lap and then called a man in to shave off the seven braids of his hair. She made him vulnerable and his strength left him. **16:20** She said, "The Philistines are here, Samson!" He woke up and thought, "I will do as I did before and shake myself free." But he did not realize that the Lord had left him. **16:21** The Philistines captured him and gouged out his eyes. They brought him down to Gaza and bound him in bronze chains. He became a grinder in the prison. **16:22** His hair began to grow back after it had been shaved off.

16:23 The rulers of the Philistines gathered to offer a great sacrifice to Dagon their god and to celebrate. They said, "Our god has handed Samson, our enemy, over to us." **16:24** When the people saw him, they praised their god, saying, "Our god has handed our enemy over to us, the one who ruined our land and killed so many of us!"

16:25 When they really started celebrating, they said, "Call for Samson so he can entertain us!" So they summoned Samson from the prison and he entertained them. They made him stand between two pillars. **16:26** Samson said to the young man who held his hand, "Position me so I can touch the pillars that support the temple. Then I can lean on them." **16:27** Now the temple was filled with men and women, and all the rulers of the Philistines were there. There were three thousand men and women on the roof watching Samson entertain. **16:28** Samson called to the Lord, "O Master, Lord, remember me! Strengthen me just one more time, O God, so I can get swift revenge against the Philistines for my two eyes!" **16:29** Samson took hold of the two middle pillars that supported the temple and he leaned against them, with his right hand on one and his left hand on the other. **16:30** Samson said, "Let me die with the Philistines!" He pushed hard and the temple collapsed on the rulers and all the people in it. He killed many more people in his death than he had killed during his life. **16:31** His brothers and all his family went down and brought him back. They buried him between Zorah and Eshtaol in the tomb of Manoah his father. He had led Israel for twenty years.

TUESDAY: SAMSON'S MOTHER

The angel appears to a barren woman who will become Samson's mother. And he provides some instructions.

1. What dietary restrictions does the angel give (13:4)?

_____

_____

_____

2. What two additional pronouncements does the angel make (13:5)?

_____

_____

_____

3. When Samson's mother reports the news to her husband (13:6–7), she omits something. What does she leave out? Notice the result in verse 12.

_____

_____

4. If you have children, what purposes has God revealed for them, and how can you as a parent pass to them a sense of purpose?

_____

_____

_____

5. What characteristics do you learn about God in the rest of chapter 13?

_____

_____

_____

WEDNESDAY: SAMSON WEAK AND STRONG

1. Re-read chapter 14, looking for evidence of the Spirit's involvement in Samson's life.

Judges 14

14:1 Samson went down to Timnah, where a Philistine girl caught his eye. **14:2** When he got home, he told his father and mother, "A Philistine girl in Timnah has caught my eye. Now get her for my wife." **14:3** But his father and mother said to him, "Certainly you can find a wife among your relatives or among all our people! You should not have to go and get a wife from the uncircumcised Philistines." But Samson said to his father, "Get her for me, because she is the right one for me." **14:4** Now his father and mother did not realize this was the Lord's doing. He was looking for an opportunity to stir up trouble with the Philistines, for at that time the Philistines were ruling Israel.

14:5 Samson went down to Timnah. When he approached the vineyards of Timnah, he saw a roaring young lion attacking him. **14:6** The Lord's spirit empowered him and he tore the lion in two with his bare hands as easily as one would tear a young goat. But he did not tell his father or mother what he had done.

14:7 Samson continued on down to Timnah and spoke to the girl. In his opinion, she was just the right one. **14:8** Some time later, when he went back to marry her, he turned aside to see the lion's remains. He saw a swarm of bees in the lion's carcass, as well as some honey. **14:9** He scooped it up with his hands and ate it as he walked along. When he returned to his father and mother, he offered them some and they ate it. But he did not tell them he had scooped the honey out of the lion's carcass.

14:10 Then Samson's father accompanied him to Timnah for the marriage. Samson hosted a party there, for this was customary for bridegrooms to do. **14:11** When the Philistines saw he had no attendants, they gave him thirty groomsmen who kept him company. **14:12** Samson said to them, "I will give you a riddle. If you really can solve it during the seven days the party lasts, I will give you thirty linen robes and thirty sets of clothes. **14:13** But if you cannot solve it, you will give me thirty linen robes and thirty sets of clothes." They said to him, "Let us hear your riddle." **14:14** He said to them, "Out of the one who eats came something to eat; out of the strong one came something sweet."

They could not solve the riddle for three days.

14:15 On the fourth day they said to Samson's bride, "Trick your husband into giving the solution to the riddle. If you refuse, we will burn up you and your father's family. Did you invite us here to make us poor?" **14:16** So Samson's bride cried on his shoulder and said, "You must hate me; you do not love me! You told the young men a riddle, but you have not told me the solution." He said to her, "Look, I have not even told my father or mother. Do you really expect me to tell you?" **14:17** She cried on his shoulder until the party was almost over. Finally, on the seventh day, he told her because she had nagged him so much. Then she told the young men the solution to the riddle. **14:18** On the seventh day, before the sun set, the men of the city said to him, "What is sweeter than honey? What is stronger than a lion?"

He said to them, "If you had not plowed with my heifer, you would not have solved my riddle!"

14:19 The Lord's spirit empowered him. He went down to Ashkelon and murdered thirty men. He took their clothes and gave them to the men who had solved the riddle. He was furious as he went back home. **14:20** Samson's bride was then given to his best man.

2. Now go back and re-read 13:24—14:6; 14:19; 15:14 (below).

Judges 13:24 Manoah's wife gave birth to a son and named him Samson. The child grew and the Lord empowered him. **13:25** The Lord's spirit began to control him in Mahaneh Dan between Zorah and Eshtaol.

14:1 Samson went down to Timnah, where a Philistine girl caught his eye. **14:2** When he got home, he told his father and mother, "A Philistine girl in Timnah has caught my eye. Now get her for my wife." **14:3** But his father and mother said to him, "Certainly you can find a wife among your relatives or among all our people! You should not have to go and get a wife from the uncircumcised Philistines." But Samson said to his father, "Get her for me, because she is the right one for me." **14:4** Now his father and mother did not realize this was the Lord's doing. He was looking for an opportunity to stir up trouble with the Philistines, for at that time the Philistines were ruling Israel.

14:5 Samson went down to Timnah. When he approached the vineyards of Timnah, he saw a roaring young lion attacking him. **14:6** The Lord's spirit empowered him and he tore the lion in two with his bare hands as easily as one would tear a young goat. But he did not tell his father or mother what he had done.

14:19 The Lord's spirit empowered him. He went down to Ashkelon and murdered thirty men. He took heir clothes and gave them to the men who had solved the riddle. He was furious as he went back home.

15:14 When [Samson] arrived in Lehi, the Philistines shouted as they approached him. But the Lord's spirit empowered him in power. The ropes around his arms were flax dissolving in fire, and they melted away from his hands.

3. At what times is the Spirit of the Lord said to be involved in Samson's life in some way?

_____

_____

_____

_____

4. Read Hebrews 11:32–33. What does it say about Samson?

> **Hebrews 11:32–33** And what more shall I say? For time will fail me if I tell of Gideon, Barak, Samson, Jephthah, of David and Samuel and the prophets. Through faith they conquered kingdoms, administered justice, gained what was promised, shut the mouths of lions.

_____

_____

_____

_____

5. What do you see as your own key spiritual strength and fleshly weakness?

_____

_____

_____

Note that while Samson hates Philistine men, he seems to think Philistine women were pretty great. In Judges 14:7–9 we read that Samson is a lion killer with a sweet tooth; he likes honey and "honeys." Yet notice that his marriage is of the Lord's doing (14:4).

In Judges 14 we read how Samson, empowered by the Spirit, kills a lion (vv. 5–6) and then later eats honey from its carcass (vv. 8–9). Both events foreshadow key episodes in the story, telling us something about Samson's strength and weakness. His lion-killing skill shows what he could accomplish through the Spirit. With God's help, he defeats one thousand Philistines, just as he kills the lion. His honey-eating episode suggests his failure to control lusts and that satisfying his physical desires is more important to him than his status as a Nazirite. (Nazirites weren't to hang around carcasses.)

6. The Holy Spirit continually came upon Samson and used him despite his lusts and weaknesses. What does this suggest to us about God? What does that say about us?

_____

_____

Take a moment to thank God for working through and loving you despite sin in your life. Then take a few more moments to deal with sins that come to mind.

THURSDAY: SAMSON AND DELILAH

Why in the world did Samson trust Delilah? Probably because she looked so fine. As was true then and is still true today, evil often comes in a great-looking package.

1. Read Judges 16:6–9.

> **Judges 16:6** So Delilah said to Samson, "Tell me what makes you so strong and how you can be subdued and humiliated." **16:7** Samson said to her, "If they tie me up with seven fresh bowstrings that have not been dried, I will become weak and be just like any other man." **16:8** So the rulers of the Philistines brought her seven fresh bowstrings which had not been dried and they tied him up with them. **16:9** They hid in the bedroom and then she said to him, "The Philistines are here, Samson!" He snapped the bowstrings as easily as a thread of yarn snaps when it is put close to fire. The secret of his strength was not discovered.

A. Summarize what happens.

_____

_____

B. Does Samson tell the truth?

_____

C. Does Delilah prove herself trustworthy?

_____

2. Read Judges 16:10–12.

> **Judges 16:10** Delilah said to Samson, "Look, you deceived me and told me lies. Now tell me how you can be subdued." **16:11** He said to her, "If they tie me tightly with brand new ropes that have never been used, I will become weak and be just like any other man." **16:12** So Delilah took new ropes and tied him with them and said to him, "The Philistines are here, Samson!" (The Philistines were hiding in the bedroom.) But he tore the ropes from his arms as if they were a piece of thread.

A. Summarize what happens.

_____

_____

_____

B. Does Samson tell the truth?

_____

C. Does Delilah prove herself trustworthy?

_____

3. Read Judges 16:13–14.

> **16:13** Delilah said to Samson, "Up to now you have deceived me and told me lies. Tell me how you can be subdued." He said to her, "If you weave the seven braids of my hair into the fabric on the loom and secure it with the pin, I will become weak and be like any other man." **16:14** So she made him go to sleep, wove the seven braids of his hair into the fabric on the loom, fastened it with the pin, and said to him, "The Philistines are here, Samson!" He woke up and tore away the pin of the loom and the fabric.

A. Summarize what happens.

_____

_____

_____

B. Does Samson tell the truth?

_____

C. Does Delilah prove herself trustworthy?

_____

D. Does Samson learn anything from the pattern he's seen in Delilah?

_____

4. Read Judges 16:15–21.

> **Judges 16:15** She said to him, "How can you say, 'I love you,' when you will not share your secret with me? Three times you have deceived me and have not told me what makes you so strong." **16:16** She nagged him every day and pressured him until he was sick to death of it. **16:17** Finally he told her his secret. He said to her, "My hair has never been cut, for I have been dedicated to God from the time I was conceived. If my head were shaved, my strength would leave me; I would become weak, and be just like all other men." **16:18** When Delilah saw that he had told her his secret, she sent for the rulers of the Philistines, saying, "Come up here again, for he has told me his secret. So the rulers of the Philistines went up to visit her, bringing the silver in their hands. **16:19** She made him go to sleep on her lap and then called a man in to shave off the seven braids of his hair. She made him vulnerable and his strength left him. **16:20** She said, "The Philistines are here, Samson!" He woke up and thought, "I will do as I did before and shake myself free." But he did not realize that the Lord had left him. **16:21** The Philistines captured him and gouged out his eyes. They brought him down to Gaza and bound him in bronze chains. He became a grinder in the prison. **16:22** His hair began to grow back after it had been shaved off.

A. Summarize what happens.

_____

_____

_____

B. Does Samson tell the truth?

_____

C. Does Delilah prove herself trustworthy?

_____

Twice in the life of Samson we read, "And he saw a woman." Later we read the same thing with King David in the Bathsheba account. Compare Judges 14:1; Judges 16:1; and 2 Samuel 11:2 below.

Judges 14:1 Samson went down to Timnah, where a Philistine girl caught his eye.

Judges 16:1 Samson went to Gaza. There he saw a prostitute and went in to have sex with her.

2 Samuel 11:2 One evening David got up from his bed and walked around on the roof of his palace. From the roof he saw a woman bathing. Now this woman was very attractive. . . .

Flagrant immorality on the part of a nation's leaders is a sign that a society is decadent.

5. Look at the negative example of Delilah, who kept a man from following God by using her sexual power. Are you using your womanliness in an unwholesome way to attract attention to yourself and satisfy your ego? If married, how can you use that same influence positively to satisfy your husband?

_____

_____

_____

1. Samson was a Nazirite. To be "nazir" was to be separate or set apart. John the Baptist was a Nazirite, which is not to be confused with being a Nazarene, someone from the city of Nazareth. Read the law as it pertained to Nazirites:

Numbers 6

6:1 Then the Lord spoke to Moses: **6:2** "Speak to the Israelites, and tell them, 'When either a man or a woman takes a special vow, to take a vow as a Nazirite, to separate himself to the Lord, **6:3** he must separate himself from wine and strong drink, he must drink neither vinegar made from wine nor vinegar made from strong drink, nor may he drink any juice of grapes, nor eat fresh grapes or dried. **6:4** All the days of his separation he must not eat anything that is produced by the grapevine, from seed to skin.

6:5 " 'All the days of the vow of his separation no razor may be used on his head until the days are fulfilled for which he separated himself to the Lord. He will be holy, and he must let the locks of the hair of his head grow.

6:6 " 'All the days that he separates himself to the Lord he must not contact a dead body. **6:7** He must not defile himself even for his father or his mother or his brother or his sister when they die, because the separation for his God is on his head. **6:8** All the days of his separation he must be holy to the Lord.

6:9 " 'If anyone dies very suddenly beside him and he defiles his consecrated head, then he must shave his head on the day of his purification—on the seventh day he must shave it. **6:10** On the eighth day he is to bring two turtledoves or two young pigeons to the priest, to the entrance to the tent of meeting. **6:11** Then the priest will offer one for a purification offering and the other as a burnt offering, and make atonement for him, because of his transgression in regard to the corpse. So he must reconsecrate his head on that day. **6:12** He must rededicate to the Lord the days of his separation and bring a male lamb in its first year as a reparation offering, but the former days will be lost because his separation was defiled.

6:13 " 'Now this is the law of the Nazirite: when the days of his separation are fulfilled, he must be brought to the entrance of the tent of meeting, **6:14** and he must present his offering to the Lord: one male lamb in its first year without blemish for a burnt offering, one ewe lamb in its first year without blemish for a purification offering, one ram without blemish for a peace offering, **6:15** and a basket of unleavened bread, cakes of fine flour mixed with olive oil, unleavened wafers smeared with olive oil, and their grain offering and their drink offerings.

6:16 "'Then the priest must present all these before the Lord and offer his purification offering and his burnt offering. **6:17** Then he must offer the ram as a peace offering to the Lord, with the basket of unleavened bread; the priest must also offer his grain offering and his drink offering.

6:18 "'Then the Nazirite must shave his consecrated head at the entrance to the tent of meeting and must take the hair from his consecrated head and put it on the fire where the peace offering is burning. **6:19** And the priest must take the boiled shoulder of the ram, one unleavened cake from the basket, and one unleavened wafer, and put them on the hands of the Nazirite after he has shaved his consecrated head; **6:20** then the priest must wave them as a wave offering before the Lord; it is a holy portion for the priest, together with the breast of the wave offering and the thigh of the raised offering. After this the Nazirite may drink wine.'

6:21 "This is the law of the Nazirite who vows to the Lord his offering of his separation, as well as whatever else he can provide. Thus he must fulfill his vow that he vows, according to the law of his separation."

2. A Nazirite had to follow some "external" laws that were to reflect his or her inner reality. List the rules regarding the following.

A. Grapes (signs of luxury)

_____

_____

_____

B. Hair

_____

_____

C. The dead

_____

_____

_____

3. Instead of fighting with Israel, the Philistines used trade and inter-
marriage to bring down their enemies. In Judges 15:6 we get a snap-
shot of the Philistines' character. What do they do?

_____

_____

_____

4. Describe the character of Samson's own people (see 15:9–13).

_____

_____

_____

5. Re-read 15:14–16:1.

> **Judges 15:14** When he arrived in Lehi, the Philistines shouted
> as they approached him. But the Lord's spirit empowered him. The
> ropes around his arms were like flax dissolving in fire, and they
> melted away from his hands. **15:15** He happened to see a solid jaw-
> bone of a donkey. He grabbed it and struck down a thousand men.
> **15:16** Samson then said,
>
> "With the jawbone of a donkey
> I have left them in heaps;
> with the jawbone of a donkey
> I have struck down a thousand men!"
>
> **15:17** When he finished speaking, he threw the jawbone down
> and named that place Ramath Lehi.
>
> **15:18** He was very thirsty, so he cried out to the Lord and said,

"You have given your servant this great victory. But now must I die of thirst and fall into hands of the Philistines?" **15:19** So God split open the basin at Lehi and water flowed out from it. When he took a drink, his strength was restored and he revived. For this reason he named the spring En Hakkore. It remains in Lehi to this very day. **15:20** Samson led Israel for twenty years during the days of Philistine prominence.

Judges 16:1 Samson went to Gaza. There he saw a prostitute and went in to have sex with her.

More space is given to Samson than any other judge. What was Samson's character like? What evidence do we have that Samson's life is full of contradictions?

_____

_____

_____

_____

God's Character

During the time of Samson, not one citizen seemed to have a heart that was consistently in tune with God's desires. Yet notice that the Lord limited how long the evil nations could oppress His children, even when they failed to repent and call out to Him. Those who portray God in the Old Testament as a stern and unforgiving God who enjoys doling out judgment are clearly missing some key elements in the text. God's people cheated on Him continually, yet He kept delivering them, even when they were not sorry.

SATURDAY: LESSONS FROM SAMSON

Scripture: "Samson called to the Lord, 'O Master, Lord, remember me! Strengthen me just one more time, O God, so I can get swift revenge against the Philistines for my two eyes!'" (Judges 16:28)

Samson's story is tragic, yet we can learn much from his mistakes. Here are some examples:

- *Sometimes we can be so focused on separation that we miss out on holiness.* Samson had ritual obedience with unbridled license—he was rigid about keeping his hair long, but he didn't hesitate to touch a dead carcass or lie with a prostitute.

It reminds me of something that happened to a friend. After Liliana placed her faith in Christ, she had a new lightness in her step. She felt the joy of a heart relieved of guilt. Yet the next time I saw her, her smile looked as deflated as a limp balloon. Apparently some Christians had given her "the list": no make-up, blue jeans, secular music, or hair worn down in tresses. The list said nothing of love, joy, peace, patience, goodness, kindness, gentleness, faithfulness, or self-control. Sometimes we wrongly define the Christian life by a list of "nots." In doing so we get rigid about sacrifice but fudge on the deeper heart matters. Remember the words of Samuel: "Obedience is better than sacrifice" (1 Sam. 15:22).

- *Often moral compromise comes in beautifully wrapped packages.* For Samson compromise came in the form of a Philistine wife, a prostitute from Gaza, and a woman named Delilah. If we think we can mess with something that attractive, we have too high a view of ourselves. Yes, we're to stand and fight when it comes to temptation—except when it involves idolatry or immorality. Then we're supposed to do what Joseph did—turn on our heels and flee (see 1 Cor. 6:18; 10:14; 2 Tim. 2:22).

- *Even our flaws can't thwart God's purposes.* Our sins and weaknesses steal our joy; they even lead us to suffering as we endure the consequences of our own actions. But they don't keep God from ultimately doing His will. Notice how at the end God took Samson's desire for revenge (rather than for God's renown) and used even that to accomplish His purpose. That's not to say Samson's weaknesses were in any way good. It's only to say we have an omnipotent and creative God who's always in control.

Samson had lots of failings. Yet his name is included in the list of heroes found in Hebrews 11. The great cloud of witnesses who have been heroes of the faith before us include Samson. He had the Holy Spirit only at limited times for limited purposes. Yet today Christian believers have the promise of the indwelling Spirit to empower them.

When you fail, admit it. Then do a one-eighty, telling God that if you had it all to do over, you would handle things differently by His grace. Tell Him you're sorry; then believe His promise to forgive you. Trust that He can and will use you, even if you've messed up. He used Samson, didn't He?

Prayer: *Thank You, Father, that even my sins and failings don't thwart Your purposes. Thank You for using me even when I'm so imperfect. Help me to see the dangers of compromise in my own life and to run the other way. Take my heart and mold it so it's tender toward You and Your will. Help me to focus on externals only as they reflect what's inside rather than as excuses to keep me from dealing with the real heart matters. Help me to follow You in such a way that those around who worship at the thrones of materialism, self, and other false gods will see Your power at work in my life and forsake those gods to worship You. In Christ's name I pray. Amen.*

For Memorization: "Manoah said to the Lord's messenger, 'Tell us your name, so we can honor you when your announcement comes true.' The Lord's messenger said to him, 'You should not ask me my name, because you cannot comprehend it.' " (Judg. 13:17–18)

Week 6 of 6

Civil War and Anarchy: Judges 17—21

Sunday: Girl Power?

Scripture: "The Benjaminites did as instructed. They abducted two hundred of the dancing girls to be their wives. They went home to their own territory, rebuilt their cities, and settled down." (Judges 21:23)

In the beginning of Judges we saw how Caleb's daughter got off her donkey, asked her father for some water, and was granted prime real estate. Now we've reached the end of Judges, where, after many downward spirals, we have seen leadership decline such that a concubine is gang-raped, cut up, and distributed throughout the land. No longer is the enemy the oppressor. God's own people terrorize each other.

Often the measure of a culture's greatness is how it treats its most vulnerable citizens. And in Judges, women are among the most vulnerable. Women will always be vulnerable in a way that men are not. A man can be raped—but not by a woman. Yet women have certainly come a long way from the ancient Near East to modern-day North America.

Most women in North America today are not powerless. Thanks to our great-grandmothers, we have the right to vote, to own property, to inherit—all rights unknown to women who lived at the time when Judges was written. In fact, the rights we have were unknown even to Martha Washington and Abigail Adams. It hasn't been all that long. Clearly much has changed in a relatively short time.

Today in Western nations women have more influence than ever. Yet what have we done with our newly-acquired power? Millions have aborted babies. Thousands have abandoned their kids. Our women's prisons are full. And the sexual power women have used to supplant men is evident from Madison Avenue to Las Vegas to Hollywood.

We're not powerless. In fact, we have the tremendous opportunity to choose between using our strong influence for good or for evil. Christ-following women have already received God's grace and enabling to wield often unseen but significant influence in our nation's homes, communities, work places, and most importantly, before God's throne.

How are we using the power, or the influence, we already have?

By God's grace . . .
- we have the power to share the gospel with a needy world.
- we have the power to forgive those who have wronged us and to give grace to those who don't deserve it.
- we have the power to offer deep joy to our families.
- we have the power to love others who are different from us.
- we have the power to care for the bereaved, single parents and their children, the sick, the dying, those who cannot give back, and those who have left all to follow Christ.
- we have the power to protect others' reputations by holding our tongues.
- we have the power to bless others with what we say.
- we have the power to help others change through loving guidance and, when necessary, even confrontation.
- we have the power to use our gifts to God's glory.
- we have the power to help develop children into well-adjusted human beings (whether they're our own or others').
- we have the power to speak boldly on behalf of the persecuted church.
- we have the power to change society through vote and voice.
- we have the power to be gentle, kind, and humble.

- we have the power to give away power so others can develop their potential.
- we have the power to pray to and thus call upon our loving Father, who places all the power in the universe at our disposal if we pray within His will.

How are we using the power we have?

MONDAY: OVERVIEW

1. Pray for insight. Then read Judges 17—21.

Judges 17

17:1 There was a man named Micah from the Ephraimite hill country. **17:2** He said to his mother, "You know the eleven hundred pieces of silver which were stolen from you, about which I heard you pronounce a curse? Look here, I have the silver. I stole it, but now I am giving it back to you." His mother said, "May the Lord reward you, my son!" **17:3** When he gave back to his mother the eleven hundred pieces of silver, his mother said, "I solemnly dedicate this silver to the Lord. It will be for my son's benefit. We will use it to make a carved image and a metal image." **17:4** When he gave the silver back to his mother, she took two hundred pieces of silver to a silversmith, who made them into a carved image and a metal image. She then put them in Micah's house. **17:5** Now this man Micah owned a shrine. He made an ephod and some personal idols and hired one of his sons to serve as a priest. **17:6** In those days Israel had no king. Each man did what he considered to be right.

17:7 There was a young man from Bethlehem in Judah. He was a Levite who had been temporarily residing among the tribe of Judah. **17:8** This man left the town of Bethlehem in Judah to find another place to live. He came to the Ephraimite hill country and made his way to Micah's house. **17:9** Micah said to him, "Where do you come from?" He replied, "I am a Levite from Bethlehem in Judah. I am looking for a new place to live." **17:10** Micah said to him, "Stay with me. Become my adviser and priest. I will give you ten pieces of silver per year, plus clothes and food." **17:11** So the Levite agreed to stay with the man; the young man was like a son to Micah. **17:12** Micah paid the Levite; the young man became his priest and lived in Micah's house. **17:13** Micah said, "Now I know God will make me rich, because I have this Levite as my priest."

Judges 18

18:1 In those days Israel had no king. And in those days the Danite tribe was looking for a place to settle, because at that time they did not yet have a place to call their own among the tribes of Israel. **18:2** The Danites sent out from their whole tribe five representatives, capable men from Zorah and Eshtaol, to spy out the land and explore it. They said to them, "Go, explore the land." They came to the Ephraimite hill country and spent the night at Micah's house. **18:3** As they approached Micah's house, they recognized the accent of the young Levite. So they stopped there and said to him, "Who brought you here? What are you doing in this place? What is your business here?" **18:4** He told them what Micah had done for him, saying, "He hired me and I became his priest." **18:5** They said to him, "Seek a divine oracle for us, so we can know if we will be successful on our mission." **18:6** The priest said to them, "Go with confidence. The Lord will be with you on your mission."

18:7 So the five men journeyed on and arrived in Laish. They noticed that the people there were living securely, like the Sidonians do, undisturbed and unsuspecting. No conqueror was troubling them in any way. They lived far from the Sidonians and had no dealings with anyone. **18:8** When the Danites returned to their tribe in Zorah and Eshtaol, their kinsmen asked them, "How did it go?" **18:9** They said, "Come on, let's attack them, for we saw their land and it is very good. You seem lethargic, but don't hesitate to invade and conquer the land." **18:10** When you invade, you will encounter unsuspecting people. The land is wide! God is handing it over to you—a place that lacks nothing on earth!"

18:11 So six hundred Danites, fully armed, set out from Zorah and Eshtaol. **18:12** They went up and camped in Kiriath Jearim in Judah. (To this day that place is called Camp of Dan. It is west of Kiriath Jearim.) **18:13** From there they traveled through the Ephraimite hill country and arrived at Micah's house. **18:14** The five men who had gone to spy out the land of Laish said to their kinsmen, "Do you realize that inside these houses are an ephod, some personal idols, a carved image, and a metal image? Decide now what you want to do." **18:15** They stopped there, went inside the young Levite's house (which belonged to Micah), and asked him how he was doing. **18:16** Meanwhile the six hundred Danites, fully armed, stood at the entrance to the gate. **18:17** The five men who had gone to spy out the land broke in and stole the carved image, the ephod, the personal idols, and the metal image, while the priest was standing at the entrance to the gate with the six hundred fully armed men. **18:18** When these men broke into Micah's house and stole the carved image, the ephod, the personal idols, and the metal image, the priest said to them, "What are you doing?" **18:19** They said to him, "Shut up! Put your hand over your mouth and come with us! You can be our adviser and priest. Wouldn't it be better to be a priest for a whole Israelite tribe than for just one man's family?" **18:20** The priest was happy. He took the ephod, the personal idols, and the carved image and joined the group.

18:21 They turned and went on their way, but they walked behind the children, the cattle, and their possessions. **18:22** After they had gone a good distance from Micah's house, Micah's neighbors gathered together and caught up with the Danites. **18:23** When they called out to the Danites, the Danites turned around and said to Micah, "Why have you gathered together?" **18:24** He said, "You stole my gods that I made, as well as this priest, and then went away. What do I have left? How can you have the audacity to say to me, 'What do you want?'" **18:25** The Danites said to him, "Don't say another word to us, or some very angry men will attack you, and you and your family will die." **18:26** The Danites went on their way; when Micah realized they were too strong to resist, he turned around and went home.

18:27 Now the Danites took what Micah had made, as well as his priest, and came to Laish, where the people were undisturbed and unsuspecting. They struck them down with the sword and burned the city. **18:28** No one came to the rescue because the city was far from Sidon and they had no dealings with anyone. The city was in a valley near Beth Rehob. The Danites rebuilt the city and occupied it. **18:29** They named it Dan after their ancestor, who was one of Israel's sons. But the city's name used to be Laish. **18:30** The Danites worshiped the carved image. Jonathan, descendant of Gershom, son of Moses, and his descendants served as priests for the tribe of Dan until the time of the exile. **18:31** They worshiped Micah's carved image the whole time God's authorized shrine was in Shiloh.

Judges 19

19:1 In those days Israel had no king. There was a Levite living temporarily in the remote region of the Ephraimite hill country. He acquired a concubine from Bethlehem in Judah. **19:2** However, she got mad at him and went home to her father's house in Bethlehem in Judah. When she had been there four months, **19:3** her husband came after her, hoping he could convince her to return. He brought with him his servant and a pair of donkeys. When she brought him into her father's house and the girl's father saw him, he warmly greeted him. **19:4** His father-in-law, the girl's father, persuaded him to stay with him for three days, and they ate and drank together, and spent the night there. **19:5** On the fourth day they woke up early and the Levite got ready to leave. But the girl's father said to his son-in-law, "Have a bite to eat for some energy, then you can go." **19:6** So the two of them sat down and had a meal together. Then the girl's father said to the man, "Why not stay another night and have a good time!" **19:7** When the man got ready to leave, his father-in-law convinced him to stay another night. **19:8** He woke up early in the morning on the fifth day so he could leave, but the girl's father said, "Get some energy. Wait until later in the day to leave!" So they ate a meal together. **19:9** When the man got ready to leave with his concubine and his servant, his father-in-law, the girl's father, said to him, "Look! The day is almost over! Stay another night! Since the day is over, stay another night here and have a good time. You can get up early tomorrow and start your trip home." **19:10** But the man did not want to stay another night. He left and traveled as far as Jebus (that is, Jerusalem). He had with him a pair of saddled donkeys and his concubine.

19:11 When they got near Jebus, it was getting quite late and the servant said to his master, "Come on, let's stop at this Jebusite city and spend the night in it." **19:12** But his master said to him, "We should not stop at a foreign city where non-Israelites live. We will travel on to Gibeah." **19:13** He said to his servant, "Come on, we will go into one of the other towns and spend the night in Gibeah or Ramah." **19:14** So they traveled on, and the sun went down when they were near Gibeah in Benjamin. **19:15** They stopped there and decided to spend the night in Gibeah. They came into the city and sat down in the town square, but no one invited them to spend the night.

19:16 But then an old man passed by, returning at the end of the day from his work in the field. The man was from the Ephraimite hill country; he was living temporarily in Gibeah. (The residents of the town were Benjaminites.) **19:17** When he looked up and saw the traveler in the town square, the old man said, "Where are you heading? Where do you come from?" **19:18** The Levite said to him, "We are traveling from Bethlehem in Judah to the remote region of the Ephraimite hill country. That's where I'm from. I had business in Bethlehem in Judah, but now I'm heading home. But no one has invited me into their home. **19:19** We have enough straw and grain for our donkeys, and there is enough food and wine for me, your female servant, and the young man who is with your servants. We lack nothing." **19:20** The old man said, "Everything is just fine! I will take care of all your needs. But don't spend the night in the town square." **19:21** So he brought him to his house and fed the donkeys. They washed their feet and had a meal.

19:22 They were having a good time, when suddenly some men of the city, some good-for-nothings, surrounded the house and kept beating on the door. They said to the old man who owned the house, "Send out the man who came to visit you so we can have sex with him." **19:23** The man who owned the house went outside and said to them, "No, my brothers! Don't do this wicked thing! After all, this man is a guest in my house. Don't do such a disgraceful thing! **19:24** Here are my virgin daughter and the visitor's concubine. I will send them out and you can abuse them and do to them whatever you like. But don't do such a disgraceful thing to this man!" **19:25** The men refused to listen to him, so the Levite grabbed his concubine and made her go outside. They raped her and abused her all night long until morning. They let her go at dawn. **19:26** The woman arrived back at daybreak and was sprawled out on the doorstep of the house where her master was staying until it became light. **19:27** When her master got up in the morning, opened the doors of the house, and went outside to start on his journey, there was the woman, his concubine, sprawled out on the doorstep of the house with her hands on the threshold. **19:28** He said to her, "Get up,

The tribe of Dan settled in the far north. When we see the phrase in the Old Testament, "All the Israelites from Dan to Beer Sheba," it means from one end of the country to the other. Though Israelite territory covered less geographic area than the U.S., saying from-Dan-to-Beer-Sheba expression was a little like an American saying "everybody from New York to L.A."

let's leave!" But there was no response. He put her on the donkey and went home. **19:29** When he got home, he took a knife, grabbed his concubine, and carved her up into twelve pieces. Then he sent them throughout Israel. **19:30** Everyone who saw the sight said, "Nothing like this has happened or been witnessed during the entire time since the Israelites left the land of Egypt. Take careful note of it! Discuss it and speak!"

Judges 20

20:1 All the Israelites from Dan to Beer Sheba and from the land of Gilead left their homes and assembled together before the Lord at

Mizpah. **20:2** The leaders of all the people from all the tribes of Israel took their places in the assembly of God's people, which numbered four hundred thousand sword-wielding foot soldiers. **20:3** The Benjaminites heard that the Israelites had gone up to Mizpah. Then the Israelites said, "Explain how this wicked thing happened!" **20:4** The Levite, the husband of the murdered woman, spoke up, "I and my concubine stopped in Gibeah of Benjamin to spend the night. **20:5** The leaders of Gibeah attacked me and at nighttime surrounded the house where I was staying. They wanted to kill me; instead they abused my concubine so badly that she died. **20:6** I grabbed hold of my concubine and carved her up and sent the pieces throughout the territory occupied by Israel, because they committed such an unthinkable atrocity in Israel. **20:7** All you Israelites, make a decision here!"

20:8 All Israel rose up in unison and said, "Not one of us will go home! Not one of us will return to his house! **20:9** Now this is what we will do to Gibeah: We will attack the city as the lot dictates. **20:10** We will take ten of every group of a hundred men from all the tribes of Israel (and a hundred of every group of a thousand, and a thousand of every group of ten thousand) to get supplies for the army. When they arrive in Gibeah of Benjamin they will punish them for the atrocity which they committed in Israel. **20:11** So all the men of Israel gathered together at the city as allies.

20:12 The tribes of Israel sent men throughout the tribe of Benjamin, saying, "How could such a wicked thing take place? **20:13** Now, hand over the good-for-nothings in Gibeah so we can execute them and purge Israel of wickedness." But the Benjaminites refused to listen to their Israelite brothers. **20:14** The Benjaminites came from their cities and assembled at Gibeah to make war against the Israelites. **20:15** That day the Benjaminites mustered from their cities twenty-six thousand sword-wielding soldiers, besides seven hundred well-trained soldiers from Gibeah. **20:16** Among this army were seven hundred specially-trained left-handed soldiers. Each one could sling a stone and hit even the smallest target. **20:17** The men of Israel (not counting Benjamin) had mustered four hundred thousand sword-wielding soldiers, every one an experienced warrior.

20:18 The Israelites went up to Bethel and asked God, "Who should lead the charge against the Benjaminites?" The Lord said, "Judah should lead." **20:19** The Israelites got up the next morning and moved against Gibeah. **20:20** The men of Israel marched out to fight Benjamin; they arranged their battle lines against Gibeah. **20:21** The Benjaminites attacked from Gibeah and struck down twenty-two thousand Israelites that day.

20:22 The Israelite army took heart and once more arranged their battle lines, in the same place where they had taken their positions the day before. **20:23** The Israelites went up and wept before the Lord until evening. They asked the Lord, "Should we again march out to fight the Benjaminites, our brothers?" The Lord said, "Attack them!" **20:24** So the Israelites marched toward the Benjaminites the next day. **20:25** The Benjaminites again attacked them from Gibeah and struck down eighteen thousand sword-wielding Israelite soldiers.

20:26 So all the Israelites, the whole army, went up to Bethel. They wept and sat there before the Lord; they did not eat anything that day until evening. They offered up burnt sacrifices and tokens of peace to the Lord. **20:27** The Israelites asked the Lord (for the ark of God's covenant was there in those days; **20:28** Phinehas son of Eleazar, son of Aaron, was serving the Lord in those days), "Should we once more march out to fight the Benjaminites our brothers, or should we quit?" The Lord said, "Attack, for tomorrow I will hand them over to you."

20:29 So Israel hid men in ambush outside Gibeah. **20:30** The Israelites attacked the Benjaminites the next day; they took their positions against Gibeah just as they had done before. **20:31** The Benjaminites attacked the army, leaving the city unguarded. They began to strike down their enemy just as they had done before. On the main roads (one leads to Bethel, the other to Gibeah) and in the field, they struck down about thirty Israelites. **20:32** Then the Benjaminites said, "They are defeated just as before." But the Israelites said, "Let's retreat and lure them away from the city into the main roads." **20:33** All the men of Israel got up from their places and took their positions at Baal Tamar, while the Israelites hiding in ambush jumped out of their places west of Gibeah. **20:34** Ten thousand men, well-trained soldiers from all Israel, then made a frontal assault against Gibeah—the battle was fierce. But the Benjaminites did not realize that disaster was at their doorstep. **20:35** The Lord annihilated Benjamin before Israel; the Israelites struck down that day 25,100 sword-wielding Benjaminites. **20:36** Then the Benjaminites saw they were defeated. The Israelites retreated before Benjamin, because they had confidence in the men they had hid in ambush outside Gibeah. **20:37** The men hiding in ambush made a mad dash to Gibeah. They attacked and put the sword to the entire city. **20:38** The Israelites and the men hiding in ambush had arranged a signal. When the men hiding in ambush sent up a smoke signal from the city, **20:39** the Israelites counter-attacked. Benjamin had begun to strike down the Israelites; they struck down about thirty men. They said, "There's no doubt about it! They are totally defeated as in the earlier battle." **20:40** But when the signal, a pillar of smoke, began to rise up from the city, the Benjaminites turned around and saw the whole city going up in a cloud of smoke that rose high into the sky. **20:41** When the Israelites turned around, the Benjaminites panicked because they could see that disaster was on their doorstep. **20:42** They retreated before the Israelites, taking the road to the wilderness. But the battle overtook them as men from the surrounding cities struck them down. **20:43** They surrounded the Benjaminites, chased them from Nohah, and annihilated them all the way to a spot east of Geba. **20:44** Eighteen thousand Benjaminites, all of them capable warriors, fell dead. **20:45** The rest turned and ran toward the wilderness, heading toward the cliff of Rimmon. But the Israelites caught five thousand of them on the main roads. They stayed right on their heels all the way to Gidom and struck down two thousand more. **20:46** That day twenty-five thousand sword-wielding Benjaminites fell in battle, all of them capable warriors. **20:47** Six hundred survivors turned and ran away to the wilderness, to the cliff of Rimmon. They stayed there four months. **20:48** The Israelites returned to the Benjaminite towns and put the sword to them. They wiped out the cities, the animals, and everything they could find. They set fire to every city in their path.

Judges 21

21:1 The Israelites had taken an oath in Mizpah, saying, "Not one of us will allow his daughter to marry a Benjaminite." **21:2** So the people came to Bethel and sat there before God until evening, weeping loudly and uncontrollably. **21:3** They said, "Why, O Lord God of Israel, has this happened in Israel?" An entire tribe has disappeared from Israel today!"

21:4 The next morning the people got up early and built an altar there. They offered up burnt sacrifices and token of peace. **21:5** The Israelites asked, "Who from all the Israelite tribes has not assembled before the Lord?" They had made a solemn oath that whoever did not assemble before the Lord at Mizpah must certainly be executed. **21:6** The Israelites regretted what had happened to their brother Benjamin. They said, "Today we cut off an entire tribe from Israel! **21:7** How can we find wives for those who are left? After all, we took an oath in the Lord's name not to give them our daughters as wives." **21:8** So they asked, "Who from all the Israelite tribes did not assemble before the Lord at Mizpah?" Now it just so happened no one from Jabesh Gilead had come to the gathering. **21:9** When they took roll call, they noticed none of the inhabitants of Jabesh Gilead were there. **21:10** So the assembly sent 12,000 capable warriors against Jabesh Gilead. They commanded them, "Go and kill with your swords the inhabitants of Jabesh Gilead, including the women and little children. **21:11** Do this: exterminate every male, as well as every woman who has had sexual relations with a male. But spare the lives of any virgins." So they did as instructed. **21:12** They found among the inhabitants of Jabesh Gilead four hundred young girls who were virgins—they had never had sexual relations with a male. They brought them back to the camp at Shiloh in the land of Canaan.

21:13 The entire assembly sent messengers to the Benjaminites at the cliff of Rimmon and assured them they would not be harmed. **21:14** The Benjaminites returned at that time, and the Israelites gave to them the women they had spared from Jabesh Gilead. But there were not enough to go around.

21:15 The people regretted what had happened to Benjamin because the Lord had weakened the Israelite tribes. **21:16** The leaders of the assembly said, "How can we find wives for those who are left? After all, the Benjaminite women have been wiped out. **21:17** The remnant of Benjamin must be preserved. An entire Israelite tribe should not be wiped out. **21:18** But we can't allow our daughters to marry them, for the Israelites took an oath, saying, 'Whoever gives a woman to a Benjaminite will be destroyed!' **21:19** However, there is an annual festival to the Lord in Shiloh, which is north of Bethel (east of the main road that goes up from Bethel to Shechem) and south of Lebonah." **21:20** So they commanded the Benjaminites, "Go hide in the vineyards, **21:21** and keep your eyes open. When you see the daughters of Shiloh coming out to dance in the celebration, jump out from the vineyards. Each one of you, catch yourself a wife from among the daughters of Shiloh and then go home to the land of Benjamin. **21:22** When their fathers or brothers come and protest to us, we'll say to them, "Do us a favor and let them be, for we could not get each one a wife through battle. Don't worry about breaking your oath! You would only be guilty if you had voluntarily given them wives."

21:23 The Benjaminites did as instructed. They abducted two hundred of the dancing girls to be their wives. They went home to their own territory, rebuilt their cities, and settled down. **21:24** Then the Israelites dispersed from there to their respective tribal and clan territories. Each went from there to his own property. **21:25** In those days Israel had no king. Each man did what he considered to be right.

2. What are you left wondering as you read these chapters? Note any observations or unanswered questions you have.

_____

_____

_____

_____

TUESDAY: MICAH AND HIS PRIEST

1. Read Judges 17:6; 21:25. Why do you think the author summarized the times this way twice?

> **Judges 17:6** In those days Israel had no king. Each man did what he considered to be right.
>
> **Judges 21:25** In those days Israel had no king. Each man did what he considered to be right.

_____

_____

_____

_____

2. Micah (not the prophet Micah) embraces spirituality, but he mixes superstition with true worship practices. What evidence do you find of his superstitions in chapter 17?

_____

_____

_____

_____

_____

3. What are some ways people today use spiritual people and practices as good-luck charms?

_____

_____

_____

_____

4. What are some of your various motives for praying? Attending church? Doing good works? Sharing your faith? Or perhaps even pursuing career ministry?

_____

_____

_____

5. Are there ways in which you're using the Lord for "good luck" instead of obeying regardless of the cost? Do you feel God owes you a good life if you attend church and tithe?

_____

_____

_____

_____

6. What are you doing that's right in your own eyes instead of what's right in God's eyes? What can you do to change that? Pray and ask for wisdom to love Him more fully and follow more obediently.

_____

_____

_____

_____

_____

WEDNESDAY: THE DANITES' MOVE

1. Re-read chapter 18.

Judges 18

18:1 In those days Israel had no king. And in those days the Danite tribe was looking for a place to settle, because at that time they did not yet have a place to call their own among the tribes of Israel. **18:2** The Danites sent out from their whole tribe five representatives, capable men from Zorah and Eshtaol, to spy out the land and explore it. They said to them, "Go, explore the land." They came to the Ephraimite hill country and spent the night at Micah's house. **18:3** As they approached Micah's house, they recognized the accent of the young Levite. So they stopped there and said to him, "Who brought you here? What are you doing in this place? What is your business here?" **18:4** He told them what Micah had done for him, saying, "He hired me and I became his priest." **18:5** They said to him, "Seek a divine oracle for us, so we can know if we will be successful on our mission." **18:6** The priest said to them, "Go with confidence. The Lord will be with you on your mission."

18:7 So the five men journeyed on and arrived in Laish. They noticed that the people there were living securely, like the Sidonians do, undisturbed and unsuspecting. No conqueror was troubling them in any way. They lived far from the Sidonians and had no dealings with anyone. **18:8** When the Danites returned to their tribe in Zorah and Eshtaol, their kinsmen asked them, "How did it go?"

18:9 They said, "Come on, let's attack them, for we saw their land and it is very good. You seem lethargic, but don't hesitate to invade and conquer the land." **18:10** When you invade, you will encounter unsuspecting people. The land is wide! God is handing it over to you—a place that lacks nothing on earth!"

18:11 So six hundred Danites, fully armed, set out from Zorah and Eshtaol. **18:12** They went up and camped in Kiriath Jearim in Judah. (To this day that place is called Camp of Dan. It is west of Kiriath Jearim.) **18:13** From there they traveled through the Ephraimite hill country and arrived at Micah's house. **18:14** The five men who had gone to spy out the land of Laish said to their kinsmen, "Do you realize that inside these houses are an ephod, some personal idols, a carved image, and a metal image? Decide now what you want to do." **18:15** They stopped there, went inside the young Levite's house (which belonged to Micah), and asked him how he was doing. **18:16** Meanwhile the six hundred Danites, fully armed, stood at the entrance to the gate. **18:17** The five men who had gone to spy out the land broke in and stole the carved image, the ephod, the personal idols, and the metal image, while the priest was standing at the entrance to the gate with the six hundred fully armed men. **18:18** When these men broke into Micah's house and stole the carved image, the ephod, the personal idols, and the metal image, the priest said to them, "What are you doing?" **18:19** They said to him, "Shut up! Put your hand over your mouth and come with us! You can be our adviser and priest. Wouldn't it be better to be a priest for a whole Israelite tribe than for just one man's family?" **18:20** The priest was happy. He took the ephod, the personal idols, and the carved image and joined the group.

18:21 They turned and went on their way, but they walked behind the children, the cattle, and their possessions. **18:22** After they had gone a good distance from Micah's house, Micah's neighbors gathered together and caught up with the Danites. **18:23** When they called out to the Danites, the Danites turned around and said to Micah, "Why have you gathered together?" **18:24** He said, "You stole my gods that I made, as well as this priest, and then went away. What do I have left? How can you have the audacity to say to me, 'What do you want?'" **18:25** The Danites said to him, "Don't say another word to us, or some very angry men will attack you, and you and your family will die." **18:26** The Danites went on their way; when Micah realized they were too strong to resist, he turned around and went home.

18:27 Now the Danites took what Micah had made, as well as his priest, and came to Laish, where the people were undisturbed and unsuspecting. They struck them down with the sword and burned the city. **18:28** No one came to the rescue because the city was far from Sidon and they had no dealings with anyone. The city was in a valley near Beth Rehob. The Danites rebuilt the city and occupied it. **18:29** They named it Dan after their ancestor, who was one of Israel's sons. But the city's name used to be Laish. **18:30** The Danites worshiped the carved image. Jonathan, descendant of Gershom, son of Moses, and his descendants served as priests for the tribe of Dan until the time of the exile. **18:31** They worshiped Micah's carved image the whole time God's authorized shrine was in Shiloh.

2. What most grieves Micah (18:24)?

_____

_____

_____

3. What evidence do we see in this chapter of the people's spiritual bankruptcy?

_____

_____

_____

_____

4. What does Judges 18:31 suggest about the people's spiritual condition?

_____

_____

_____

_____

> "We tend to see abuse of religion go to two extremes; either people try to manipulate God with it (as we see here) or they try to manipulate others. When men and women get their hands on religion, one of the first things they often do is turn it into an instrument for controlling others, either putting or keeping them 'in their place.' The history of such religious manipulation and coercion is long and tedious. It is little wonder that people who have only known religion on such terms experience release or escape from it as freedom. The problem is that the freedom turns out to be short-lived."
>
> —Eugene Peterson, NT, Introduction to Galatians in The Message

5. Think back to the events at the beginning of Judges. Compare the nation's spiritual state to what it is now. What's different? Are the people getting better or worse?

_____

_____

_____

_____

_____

THURSDAY: POWER AND CORRUPTION

1. Re-read Judges 19.

Judges 19

19:1 In those days Israel had no king. There was a Levite living temporarily in the remote region of the Ephraimite hill country. He acquired a concubine from Bethlehem in Judah. **19:2** However, she got mad at him and went home to her father's house in Bethlehem in Judah. When she had been there four months, **19:3** her husband came after her, hoping he could convince her to return. He brought with him his servant and a pair of donkeys. When she brought him into her father's house and the girl's father saw him, he warmly greeted him. **19:4** His father-in-law, the girl's father, persuaded him to stay with him for three days, and they ate and drank together, and spent the night there. **19:5** On the fourth day they woke up early and the Levite got ready to leave. But the girl's father said to his son-in-law, "Have a bite to eat for some energy, then you can go." **19:6** So the two of them sat down and had a meal together. Then the girl's father said to the man, "Why not stay another night and have a good time!" **19:7** When the man got ready to leave, his father-in-law convinced him to stay another night. **19:8** He woke up early in the morning on the fifth day so he could leave, but the girl's father said, "Get some energy. Wait until later in the day to leave!" So they ate a meal together. **19:9** When the man got ready to leave with his concubine and his servant, his father-in-law, the girl's father, said to him, "Look! The day is almost over! Stay another night! Since the day is over, stay another night here and have a good time. You can get up early tomorrow and start your trip home." **19:10** But the man did not want to stay another night. He left and traveled as far as Jebus (that is, Jerusalem). He had with him a pair of saddled donkeys and his concubine.

19:11 When they got near Jebus, it was getting quite late and the servant said to his master, "Come on, let's stop at this Jebusite city and spend the night in it." **19:12** But his master said to him, "We should not stop at a foreign city where non-Israelites live. We will travel on to Gibeah." **19:13** He said to his servant, "Come on, we will go into one of the other towns and spend the night in Gibeah or Ramah." **19:14** So they traveled on, and the sun went down when they were near Gibeah in Benjamin. **19:15** They stopped there and decided to spend the night in Gibeah. They came into the city and sat down in the town square, but no one invited them to spend the night.

19:16 But then an old man passed by, returning at the end of the day from his work in the field. The man was from the Ephraimite hill country; he was living temporarily in Gibeah. (The residents of the town were Benjaminites.) **19:17** When he looked up and saw the traveler in the town square, the old man said, "Where are you heading? Where do you come from?" **19:18** The Levite said to him, "We are traveling from Bethlehem in Judah to the remote region of the Ephraimite hill country. That's where I'm from. I had business in Bethlehem in Judah, but now I'm heading home. But no one has invited me into their home. **19:19** We have enough straw and grain for our donkeys, and there is enough food and wine for me, your female servant, and the young man who is with your servants. We lack nothing." **19:20** The old man said, "Everything is just fine! I will take care of all your needs. But don't spend the night in the town square." **19:21** So he brought him to his house and fed the donkeys. They washed their feet and had a meal.

19:22 They were having a good time, when suddenly some men of the city, some good-for-nothings, surrounded the house and kept beating on the door. They said to the old man who owned the house, "Send out the man who came to visit you so we can have sex with him." **19:23** The man who owned the house went outside and said to them, "No, my brothers! Don't do this wicked thing! After all, this man is a guest in my house. Don't do such a disgraceful thing! **19:24** Here are my virgin daughter and the visitor's concubine. I will send them out and you can abuse them and do to them whatever you like. But don't do such a disgraceful thing to this man!" **19:25** The men refused to listen to him, so the Levite grabbed his concubine and made her go outside. They raped her and abused her all night long until morning. They let her go at dawn. **19:26** The woman arrived back at daybreak and was sprawled out on the doorstep of the house where her master was staying until it became light. **19:27** When her master got up in the morning, opened the doors of the house, and went outside to start on his journey, there was the woman, his concubine, sprawled out on the doorstep of the house with her hands on the threshold. **19:28** He said to her, "Get up, let's leave!" But there was no response. He put her on the donkey and went home. **19:29** When he got home, he took a knife, grabbed his concubine, and carved her up into twelve pieces. Then he sent them throughout Israel. **19:30** Everyone who saw the sight said, "Nothing like this has happened or been witnessed during the entire time since the Israelites left the land of Egypt. Take careful note of it! Discuss it and speak!"

2. Back during Deborah's conquest, in Judges 5:24–30 we saw sexual irony. (Sisera's mother envisioned her son raping Israel's women as the spoils of war while he actually lay dead between Jael's feet.) What has happened in the chapter you just read? How do Israelite men treat their own nation's women?

_____

_____

_____

_____

3. Read Judges 19:11–13. Why did the master not want to spend the night in this city, and where did he want to go (see vv. 12–13 below)?

> **Judges 19:11** When they got near Jebus, it was getting quite late and the servant said to his master, "Come on, let's stop at this Jebusite city and spend the night in it." **19:12** But his master said to him, "We should not stop at a foreign city where non-Israelites live. We will travel on to Gibeah." **19:13** He said to his servant, "Come on, we will go into one of the other towns and spend the night in Gibeah or Ramah."

_____

_____

_____

4. According to Judges 19:16–20, where did the man and his concubine end up staying?

> **Judges 19:16** But then an old man passed by, returning at the end of the day from his work in the field. The man was from the Ephraimite hill country; he was living temporarily in Gibeah. (The residents of the town were Benjaminites.) **19:17** When he looked up and saw the traveler in the town square, the old man said, "Where are you heading? Where do you come from?" **19:18** The Levite said to him, "We are traveling from Bethlehem in Judah to the remote region of the Ephraimite hill country. That's where I'm from. I had business in Bethlehem in Judah, but now I'm heading home. But no one has invited me into their home. **19:19** We have enough straw and grain for our donkeys, and there is enough food and wine for me, your female servant, and the young man who is with your servants. We lack nothing." **19:20** The old man said, "Everything is just fine! I will take care of all your needs. But don't spend the night in the town square."

_____

_____

_____

5. Considering what happens in Gibeah to the travelers, what is ironic about their choice to stay in "friendly" territory?

_____

_____

_____

_____

6. Re-read chapters 20–21. What does the people's treatment of fellow Israelites and women indicate about their spiritual condition?

_____

_____

_____

_____

FRIDAY: HANNAH

What is Hannah doing at the end of a study of Judges? Isn't her story in 1 Samuel?

Hannah's story takes place during the time of the Judges, and to appreciate some of the specifics in Judges, we need to read Hannah's story next.

1. Read 1 Samuel 1—2. Notice that it mirrors the structure we saw with Deborah—history followed by a poetic account.

1 Samuel 1

1:1 There was a man from Ramathaim Zuphim, from the hill country of Ephraim, whose name was Elkanah. He was the son of Jeroham, the son of Elihu, the son of Tohu, the son of Zuph, an Ephraimite. **1:2** He had two wives; the name of the first was Hannah and the name of the second was Peninnah. Now Peninnah had children, but Hannah was childless.

1:3 Year after year this man would go up from his city to worship and to sacrifice to the Lord of hosts at Shiloh. It was there that the two sons of Eli, Hophni and Phineas, served as the Lord's priests. **1:4** Whenever the day came for Elkanah to sacrifice, he used to give meat portions to his wife Peninnah and to all her sons and daughters. **1:5** But he would give a double portion to Hannah, because he especially loved her. Now the Lord had not enabled her to have children. **1:6** Her rival wife used to upset her and make her worry, for the Lord had not enabled her to have children. **1:7** Peninnah would behave this way year after year. Whenever Hannah went up to the Lord's house, Peninnah would upset her so that she would weep and not eat. **1:8** Finally Elkanah her husband said to her, "Hannah, why do you weep and not eat? Why are you so sad? Am I not better to you than ten sons?"

1:9 On one occasion in Shiloh, after they had finished eating and drinking, Hannah got up. (Now at the time Eli the priest was sitting in his chair by the doorpost of the Lord's temple.) **1:10** She was very upset as she prayed to the Lord, and she was weeping uncontrollably. **1:11** She made a vow saying, "O Lord of hosts, if you will look with compassion on the suffering of your female servant, remembering me and not forgetting your servant, and give a male child to your servant, then I will dedicate him to the Lord all the days of his life. His hair will never be cut."

1:12 As she continued praying to the Lord, Eli was watching her mouth. **1:13** Now Hannah was speaking from her heart. Although her lips were moving, her voice was inaudible. Eli therefore thought she was drunk. **1:14** So he said to her, "How often do you intend to get drunk? Put away your wine!"

1:15 But Hannah replied, "That's not the way it is, my lord! I am under a great deal of stress. I have drunk neither wine nor beer. Rather, I have poured out my soul to the Lord. **1:16** Don't consider your servant a wicked woman, for until now I have spoken from my deep pain and anguish."

1:17 Eli replied, "Go in peace, and may the God of Israel grant the request that you have asked of him." **1:18** She said, "May I, your servant, find favor in your sight." So the woman went her way and got something to eat. Her face no longer looked sad.

1:19 They got up early the next morning and after worshiping the Lord, they returned to their home at Ramah. Elkanah had marital relations with his wife Hannah, and the Lord remembered her. **1:20** After some time Hannah became pregnant and gave birth to a son. She named him Samuel, thinking, "I asked the Lord for him.

1:21 This man Elkanah went up with all his family to make the yearly sacrifice to the Lord and to keep his vow, **1:22** but Hannah did not go up. Instead she said to her husband, "Once the boy is weaned, I will bring him and appear before the Lord, and he will remain there from then on."

1:23 So her husband Elkanah said to her, "Do what you think best. Stay until you have weaned him. May the Lord fulfill his promise." So the woman stayed and nursed her son until she had weaned him. **1:24** Once she had weaned him, she took him up with her, along with three bulls, an ephah of flour, and a container of wine. She brought him to the Lord's house at Shiloh, even though he was young. **1:25** Once the bull had been slaughtered, they brought the boy to Eli. **1:26** She said, "Just as surely as you are alive, my lord, I am the woman who previously stood here with you in order to pray to the Lord. **1:27** I prayed for this boy, and the Lord has given me the request that I asked of him. **1:28** Now I dedicate him to the Lord. From this time on he is dedicated to the Lord." Then they worshiped the Lord there.

1 Samuel 2

2:1 Hannah prayed, "My heart rejoices in the Lord; my horn is exalted high because of the Lord. I loudly denounce my enemies, for I am happy that you delivered me.

2:2 No one is holy like the Lord! There is no one other than you! There is no rock like our God!

2:3 Don't keep speaking so arrogantly, letting proud talk come out of your mouth. For the Lord is a God who knows; he evaluates what people do.

2:4 The bows of warriors are shattered, but those who stumble find their strength reinforced.

2:5 Those who are well-fed hire themselves out to earn food, but the hungry no longer lack. Even the barren woman gives birth to seven, but the one with lots of children withers away.

What does it mean when Hannah says "my horn is exalted high" (2:1)? Have you ever seen horned animals fighting? Perhaps not up close, but on television? Picture those animals and consider how they use their horns both to attack and to defend themselves. Sometime they hold their heads high to display their virility and to intimidate with their strength. Hannah appears to be picturing herself as such an animal. She's giving the Lord credit for vindicating her in the presence of her "attackers."

2:6 The Lord both kills and gives life; he brings down to the grave and raises up.

2:7 The Lord impoverishes and makes wealthy; he humbles and exalts.

2:8 He lifts the weak from the dust; he raises the poor from the ash heap to seat them with princes and to bestow on them an honored position. The foundations of the earth belong to the Lord, and he has placed the world on them.

2:9 He watches over his holy ones, but the wicked are made speechless in the darkness, for it is not by one's own strength that one prevails.

2:10 The Lord shatters his adversaries; he thunders against them from the heavens. The Lord executes judgment to the ends of the earth. He will strengthen his king and exalt the power of his anointed one."

2:11 Then Elkanah went back home to Ramah. But the boy was serving the Lord under the supervision of Eli the priest.

2:12 The sons of Eli were wicked men. They did not recognize the Lord's authority. **2:13** Now the priests would always treat the people in the following way: Whenever anyone was making a sacrifice, while the meat was boiling, the priest's attendant would come with a three-pronged fork in his hand. **2:14** He would jab it into the basin, kettle, caldron, or pot, and everything that the fork brought up the priest would take for himself. This is what they used to do to all the Israelites when they came there to Shiloh.

2:15 Even before they burned the fat, the priest's attendant would come and say to the person who was making the sacrifice, "Hand over some meat for the priest to roast. He won't take boiled meat from you, but only uncooked." **2:16** If the individual said to him, "First let the fat be burned away, and then take for yourself whatever you wish," he would say, "No! Hand it over right now! If you don't, I will take it forcibly!"

2:17 The sin of these young men was very great in the Lord's sight, for they treated the Lord's offering with contempt.

2:18 Now Samuel was ministering before the Lord. The boy was dressed in a linen ephod. **2:19** His mother used to make him a small robe and bring it up to him at regular intervals when she would go up with her husband to make the annual sacrifice. **2:20** Eli would bless Elkanah and his wife saying, "May the Lord raise up for you descendants from this woman to replace the one that she dedicated to the Lord." Then they would go to their home. **2:21** So the Lord graciously attended to Hannah, and she was able to conceive and gave birth to three sons and two daughters. The boy Samuel grew up at the Lord's sanctuary.

2:22 Now Eli was very old when he heard about everything that his sons used to do to all the people of Israel and how they used to have sex with the women who were stationed at the entrance to the tent of meeting. **2:23** He said to them, "Why do you behave in this way? For I hear about these evil things from all these people. **2:24** This ought not to be, my sons! For the report that I hear circulating among the Lord's people is not good. **2:25** If a man sins against a man, one may appeal to God on his behalf. But if a man sins against the Lord, who will then pray for him?" But they would not listen to their father, for the Lord had decided to kill them.

2:26 Now the boy Samuel was growing up and finding favor both with the Lord and with men.

2:27 A man of God came to Eli and said to him, "This is what the Lord says: 'Did I not plainly reveal myself to your ancestor's house when they were in Egypt in the house of Pharaoh? **2:28** I chose your ancestor from all the tribes of Israel to be my priest, to offer sacrifice on my altar, to burn incense, and to bear the ephod before me. I gave to your ancestor's house all the fire offerings made by the Israelites. **2:29** Why are you scorning my sacrifice and my offering that I commanded for my dwelling place? You have honored your sons more than you have me in that you have made yourselves fat from the best parts of all the offerings of my people Israel.'

2:30 Therefore the Lord, the God of Israel, says, 'I really did say that your house and your ancestor's house would serve me forever.' But now the Lord says, 'May it never be! For I will honor those who honor me, but those who despise me will be cursed! **2:31** In fact, days are coming when I will remove your strength and the strength of your father's house. There will not be an old man in your house! **2:32** You will see trouble in my dwelling place. Israel will experience blessings, but there will not be an old man in your house for all time. **2:33** The man that I do not cut off from my altar, I will cause your eyes to fail and will cause you grief. All of those born to your family will die in the prime of life. **2:34** This will be a confirming sign for you that will be fulfilled through your two sons, Hophni and Phinehas: in a single day they both will die! **2:35** Then I will raise up for myself a faithful priest. He will do what is in my heart and soul. I will build for him a secure dynasty and he will serve my chosen one for all time. **2:36** Everyone who remains in your house will come to bow before him for a payment of money and for a piece of bread. Each will say, 'Assign me to a priestly task so I can eat a piece of bread.'"

2. Hannah's story takes place during the time when judges ruled Israel. From our past weeks in Judges, what do you know about the nation's spiritual state at the time?

_____

_____

_____

_____

3. How does Hannah's spiritual state differ from those in the nation around her?

_____

_____

_____

4. What are some ways in which you, like Hannah, must trust God as you stand alone against a culture—whether the culture at large or even difficult church or family relationships—and be different from the world around you?

_____

_____

_____

_____

5. At a time when the nation was at its worse, the Lord miraculously raised up a prophet and judge. Samuel went on to anoint Saul and eventually David as king of Israel. Even when the nation didn't appear to be crying out to God for help, He was working on their behalf, keeping His promises, providing a spiritually strong leader—the son of an infertile woman who trusted Him against all odds. What does this tell you about God?

_____

_____

_____

SATURDAY: A WOMAN WHOSE NAME ENDURES

Scripture: "So Samuel led Israel all the days of his life." (1 Samuel 7:15)

Have you ever memorized the books of the Bible? If so, you know that when you get to the section near Judges, the order goes like this: Joshua-Judges-Ruth-1 Samuel. Because Ruth stands between Judges and 1 Samuel, we usually follow Judges with Ruth as we read through the Bible. Perfectly logical. Yet just once we need to follow Judges with 1 Samuel, because in doing so we see a vital connection between the end of Judges and the story of Hannah and her son.

Remember how the story of Samson's mother began? "There was a man named Manoah from Zorah, from the Danite tribe. His wife was infertile and childless" (Judg. 13:2). And remember how we learned about Micah's mother? "There was a man named Micah from the Ephraimite hill country. He said to his mother. . . ." (Judg. 17:1–2).

Hannah's story begins similarly: "There was a man from Ramathaim Zuphim, from the hill country of Ephraim, whose name was Elkanah. He was the son of Jeroham . . ." (1 Sam. 1:1). Except this time we learn some names: "He had two wives; the name of the first was Hannah and the name of he second was Peninnah. Now Peninnah had children, but Hannah was childless" (1 Sam. 1:2).

Like Samson's mother and Micah's mother, Hannah lived during the time of the judges. At that time, the people were so decadent that a concubine traveling with her master was gang-raped and left dead on a doorstep. Her master took her home, cut her into twelve pieces, and sent the parts all over Israel (Judg. 19:29–30). If ever the nation needed a godly leader, this would be the time. What a sick world!

Hannah and her husband worshiped Yahweh while the people around them lived in utter decadence, even offering sacrifices to Baal. Imagine an infertile woman in that day refusing to worship Baal. Can't you just hear her neighbors? "Duh. Of course you're infertile—you've hacked off the fertility god!"

Hannah prayed in bitterness of soul with anguished tears. Then she made a vow that if God would give her a male child, she would give him back to the Lord. Even the priest didn't understand her. When he saw her lips moving in prayer, he though she must be drunk. Was it that rare to see someone praying?

Hannah's story didn't end with the answer to her prayers for a baby. She understood what Manoah's wife did not—that the "happy ending" was only the beginning of God's purpose in her son's life. Often we observe that Hannah got what she wanted, and in reading the story that way, we fail to see what it cost her to be a part of God's ongoing plan.

When Hannah's little boy, Samuel, reached his toddler years, she said, "Now I give him to the Lord." Then she wrote a lovely hymn proclaiming, "There is none holy like the Lord!" She saw her son only once a year after that—an astounding sacrifice on her part. Yet she also saw him grow up to provide the spiritual direction sorely lacking in a nation full of people compelled to do what was "right in their own eyes."

We see in Hannah a woman who trusted God through her pain. The Lord's ultimate answer required sacrifice on her part, yet she depended on Him and obeyed. And against the dark backdrop of sin in the nation, when it looked as if God had every reason to walk out on His people, He raised up Hannah's son as a righteous prophet and judge.

Hebrew scholar Robert Chisholm summarizes it this way:

> In Judges through 1 Samuel, the unnamed mothers of Samson and Micah are foils for Hannah. In contrast to Samson's mother, whose miraculously conceived Nazirite son failed to realize his potential, Hannah supernaturally gave birth to a Nazirite son through whom the Lord restored effective leadership to Israel. In contrast to Micah's mother, whose misguided zeal gave rise to a polluted, unauthorized cult, Hannah's devotion to the Lord led to the revival of genuine

[worship of the true God] through the spiritual direction provided by her son Samuel. The three accounts even begin the same way."[5]

At a time when the nation was at its worst, God had mercy. At a time when He had every reason to slam the door and never return, He raised up someone to lead the wandering nation, a man zealous for the glory of the Lord. As we observed last week, those who portray God in the Old Testament as angry and set on destroying people have definitely missed some key observations from the text. This is a God who is tenacious in drawing His people to himself even as they try to push Him away.

The Book of Judges ends at a point in the cycle when the people's "supplications" or "prayers" are no longer even offered. We see only sin and suffering, then salvation. Yet 1 Samuel tells us the story doesn't end there.

When God's people reached the point at which they didn't have the sense to plead with the Lord to rescue them, He reached out in His mercy and raised up a woman bent low. Through her He sent deliverance. He kept His promise never to leave or forsake His people—a promise He makes to us as well. That's just the kind of God He is.

Isn't He good? Will you trust Him?

Prayer: *Thank You, gracious Heavenly Father, for Your timeless Word. Thank You that the stories of Your people long ago are still a part of our story today. Thank You that when the nation of Israel turned their backs on You, You never walked away. Instead, You always kept Your promises. You showed Your grace even when they couldn't see how much they needed it—not only at the time of the judges but ultimately through the life of Your Son, our Lord. Thank You that You promise Your children today that You will never leave us or ever forsake us. I need You, Lord. Like the children of Israel, I'm prone to wander, to forget to pray, to toy with temptation, to focus on earthly pursuits and take my eyes off what really lasts. Give me the wisdom and decisiveness I need to follow You no matter what. There is no one holy like You—there is no Rock like our God. In the name of Your Son I pray. Amen.*

For Memorization: "No one is holy like the Lord! There is no one other than you. There is no rock like our God!" (1 Samuel 2:2)

---

[5] Dr. Bob Chisholm, Old Testament Introduction class notes, Dallas Theological Seminary, Spring 2001.